JUBILEE, WEALTH & THE MARKET

A NEW BEGINNING

A Call For Jubilee

Canadian Ecumenical Jubilee Initiative
1999

Jubilee, Wealth and the Market

To order copies of this book or other Jubilee materials contact your denominational office/bookstore. You can also contact:
Canadian Ecumenical Jubilee Initiative
P.O. Box 772, Station F
Toronto, ON, Canada M4Y 2N6
Tel: 416 922 1592 ext. 30   Fax: 416 922 0957
E-mail: jubilee@devp.org
Website: www.web.net/~jubilee

Cover design: Dinah Greenberg, NOMAD Design
Cover Graphic: Carolina Echeverria
Jubilee Graphic: Joyce Crosby
Editing and text layout: John Mihevc
ISBN: 0-9683714-2-6

Published 1999

Table of Contents

Introduction: Signposts for a Jubilee People................................1
   John Mihevc

The Bible, Wealth and the Market

1. "There must then be no poor among you"............................5
   Michel Beaudin

2. Jubilee Revisited: A Reflection..13
   Paul Hansen

3. The Gospel of Jesus According to Luke 25
   Maria Teresa Porcile Santiso

4. Practising Jubilee: Leviticus 25 and Luke 4:16-30.............33
   Edwin Searcy

5. The Unforgiving Servant or the Forgiving King.................39
   Sylvia C. Keesmaat

6. Reflections on the Economic Model in Light of
   Luke 19:11-27 47
   Alejandro Zorzin

7. An Outcast's Vision..53
   Joanne Clarke

8. The Homicidal Vineyard Workers.....................................61
   Richard Renshaw

Engendering Jubilee

9. A Jubilee Call for African Women 63
   Omega Bula

10. Jubilaction: Engaging with a Feminist Jubilee in a Multi-Faith and
   Secular Context 77
   Denise Nadeau and Laurel Dykstra

11. Jubilee at the Turn of the 21st Century and the
   African Woman...113
   Puleng Lenka-Bula

Confronting Market Values

12. Towards a New Jubilee Covenant 129
    Jubilee South

13. Nurturing a Spirit of Social Conversion 137
    Michel Andraos

14. Good News to the Poor: Background Paper on the Bible, Poverty,
    and Government in Contemporary Canada 141
    Evangelical Fellowship of Canada

15. Loosening the Cords that Bind Us: Reflections on a Theology
    of Debt 161
    Mark Hathaway

16. To Call the Sabbath a Delight: Lesbian and Gay Pride in the
    Jubilee Tradition.. 175
    Lionel Ketola

17. Christian Faith and Globalisation.. 181
    Jung Mo Sung

Introduction

Signposts for a Jubilee People

John Mihevc

At this moment in history, we are inspired by the Jubilee hope that wealth can be directed toward the common good of humanity within a renewed creation. — Jubilee Pledge

When we first set out on the Jubilee journey, the Canadian Ecumenical Jubilee Initiative had no idea how profound the commitment to carrying this message of hope would be. In many ways the call to be hopeful has acted like a compass, keeping us on course so that we might honour our commitment to following the jubilee path.

While the contributions in this book offer diverse understandings and approaches to what it means to be on this journey, there are four key directions that provide the bearings for reflection and action. First, they are united in a commitment to a fundamental redistribution of wealth in all its forms. Second, they are rooted in the biblical vision of Jubilee, which echoes throughout the Scriptures. Third, they speak to our own present context of debt slavery, market idolatry and the gross disparity between rich and poor. Finally, they are committed to following a vision that is forward looking, where those on the journey are always scanning the horizon in the belief that jubilee is possible and attainable.

As you accompany the contributors the following signposts help mark what it means to be a jubilee people on the move toward the new millennium.

1. The economy is a sacrament which must be ordered with a logic of gratuitousness and gift.

The biblical vision is one that insists on the precedence of the community over obedience to market laws, of *koinonia* over property. The opening contribution from Michel Beaudin and the Quebec Jubilee coalition articulates this message very clearly. In contrast, Omega Bula describes the completely opposing values of globalisation which emphasizes private over community values. This has led to the further marginalization and exclusion of women by robbing them of their community survival skills. We are challenged to live out this vision of the economy as a Jubilee people. Not only is the Bible filled with stories of Jubilee economics in action, so too is our history as Nadeau and Dykstra demonstrate. In many instances they are stories of women's resistance and living out a jubilee-inspired alternative.

2. Wealth and poverty are core issues in the Bible.

As the Evangelical Fellowship of Canada challenges us: "Poverty can never be a secondary concern for Christians since it strikes close to the heart of what it means for humans to image God." Many of the reflections consider the strong condemnations in numerous biblical passages of economic systems and practices which lead to the unchecked amassing of wealth at the expense of the poor. When we turn wealth into our God we become a powerless and impotent people. God's command that there "be no poor among you, (Deut. 15.4)" stands as a challenge and condemnation for us today.

3. The Bible condemns economic violence.

As Alejandro Zorzin notes in his reflection on Luke "the gospel rejects the savage logic of economic efficiency." As people of faith we are challenged to question the logic of neo-liberalism and market idolatry being imposed precisely because the effects are so devastating. Like Hagar, adds Joanne Clarke, we must not sit and watch the children die. The market is not God and our responsibility is to live out an alternative way, the vision of Jubilee. Many of the contributions suggest that a counter-force to neo-liberalism is beginning to emerge. People around the world are rejecting the notion that there are no alternatives and are pushing back with their own vision.

The visioning of alternatives must include a church that is willing to reclaim its prophetic role and denounce the death-dealing forces of globalisation and neo-liberalism. And yet we must do this recognising that we are living in a time of exile where there is a diversity of opinions on the way forward. Some of these spring from Jubilee's "shadow side" rooted in imperial consciousness, Paul Hansen reminds us. This is especially true for women and people of other faiths who do not seem to be the beneficiaries of Jubilee principles and in some respects are worse off in their application. Does Jubilee address the needs of women and children living with HIV/AIDs? How does debt cancellation translate to the lives of marginalized Africans asks Puleng Lenka-Bula?

4. Wealth is a form of blindness which must be converted to responsibility.

The international Jubilee movement has learned the importance of building a movement from below as well as taking its message to the world's economic leaders. Like Jesus in his attitude toward Zacchacus, we must be open to the surprise of converting those blinded by market idolatry to Jubilee responsibility notes Maria Teresa Porcile Santiso. However, Matthew 21 reminds us that those who are in charge of the vineyard are incapable of even hearing the call to change. The stories of Zacchaeus and the homicidal vineyard workers illustrate the tensions and contradictions we face with today's world leaders. Most of them are incapable of hearing the call to change yet every now and then a Zacchaeus emerges from their midst.

Conversion to Jubilee takes place in a series of small steps. It begins with Sabbath-keeping explains Edwin Searcy. Or as Sylvia Keesmaat describes, "Jubilee is beyond our expectations but not beyond our wildest hopes." Collecting 17 million petitions worldwide in the last year was beyond our expectations but certainly not beyond our wildest hopes. The response from the world's leaders was well below our expectations but nonetheless an important small step. Who knows where this will lead?

We are reminded by Jubilee South that we should not get caught up in the millennium whirlwind of campaigns. The Jubilee challenge is an ongoing one that must continue long after the year 2000.

An integral part of conversion to Jubilee is the need for a "time apart." Lionel Ketola challenges us to think of Jubilee as a time of "restructuring our economic and social relationships." This allows Jubilee to permeate all of our personal, social and economic relationships. It means to examine both the personal and structural forces that lead us away from right relations to economic disparity, racism, homophobia and gender discrimination. How completely opposite to the dominant understanding of global capitalism where, as Jung Mo Sung describes, "social inequality is the powerhouse of economic progress." In this worldview the attempt to seek solutions to social problems is both a personal sin and a sin for the state as it will only undermine the efficient functioning of the market.

In response, Michel Andraos explores the idea of "social conversion." We need to ask what the conditions are for social conversion in our time especially in the face of our pathological devotion to the market. This requires looking at the world with the eyes of faith, and collectively affirm the signs of hope in our midst. Rereading the Bible with Jubilee eyes calls us to respond in new and creative ways to the injustices we confront.

5. Forgiveness of sins in the Bible is inextricably tied to the release of debts and economic justice.

The Lord's prayer stands in radical opposition to prevailing market idolatry. Just as Jesus calls upon us to release debts we are challenged by Jubilee South to support them in their call for the repudiation of debts. Mark Hathaway probes the Lord's prayer and uncovers a number of Jubilee themes. The forgiveness of debts in the Lord's Prayer strongly implies the disentangling of the threads that strangle a relationship. Moreover, the debts we are to forgive, it is suggested, were never ours in the first place. Debt and compound interest are cords around the world's poor and the Earth. The logic of compound interest, a human construct, is the basis for which God's creation is being destroyed at an unprecedented rate. Echoing Isaiah 5, Richard Renshaw warns that, "in the current context, the entire vineyard may be destroyed! Ours is a tiny, fragile planet." The cords of debt are combined with those of structural adjustment programs or austerity measures forced on the poor which strangle them and the Earth. To be a Jubilee people is to struggle to sever these cords.

The commitment to being a Jubilee people is both a personal and collective journey. Moreover, it is not bound by the traditional campaign logic of being tied to a particular calendar year. As the Jubilee South reminds us, "the struggle for global economic and social justice has no time limit." We are in it for the long haul confident of God's presence in our steps towards becoming a Jubilee people.

1

"There must then be no poor among you"[1]

Michel Beaudin[2]

Last June a coalition of organizations presented the G-8 with one of the largest petitions in history which included more than seventeen million signatures. Six hundred thousand of these were from people all across Canada. The goal of the petition was to pressure the political and financial decision-makers into canceling the debt of the poorest nations, since the majority of the citizens had never benefited from these moneys and had already paid back the interest many times over (excluding the capital) forcing them to live in quasi-slavery.

Cancelling debts in times of social crises is not something new. It is a tradition that dates back before the sixth century of our era, to the time of the Laws of Solon in Greece. The cancelling of debts, which is the *first prescription* of the Jubilee tradition and a reminder to both Christians and Jews alike, was initiated in Israel some 3000 years ago. The people of that time agreed that they would periodically suspend economic laws whenever they threatened human life and dignity, in other words, the cohesiveness of the community, would always take precedence. According to the Law of Moses loans would 'die out' every fifty years so as to liberate those families who, because of their indebtedness, were forced to live a life of slavery.

The Quebec Jubilee Coalition is now considering the *second prescription* of the Jubilee tradition which has to do with the redistribution and access to wealth, one just as important today as it was then. We will begin by looking at how economic policy, takes precedence over the community of citizens, which makes society no longer a community of citizens but rather a market, with few winners and countless losers, takes precedence over the community of citizens. This situation is the result of the *unjust distribution* of wealth, where an upside-down *redistribution* makes things worse instead of making them better. The capitalistic West in this case appears "barbaric" when compared to those we call "primitive people." For example, the

---

[1] Dt. 15.4

[2] In collaboration with the *Coalition québécoise du Jubilé* (Quebec Jubilee Coalition).

Tsembaga of New Guinea and the First Nations on the West Coast of Canada[3] have invented rituals for the redistribution of accumulated goods so that they could be freer to live in conformity to the true spirit of equality and solidarity. The sacralization of the market, of money and of private property to the point of sacrificing entire populations, might one day be classified as "crimes against humanity." And yet the spirit of generosity of the people is still very much alive. That is why, in the second part of this article, we will turn to Scripture to see how we are called to be counter-cultural, and how it is essential for us to institutionalize the practice of gratuitousness and solidarity, without which the social "WE" cannot possibly exist.

The concentration and privatisation of the earth's wealth

In the 1950s (at least in the North) capitalism seemed to undergo a type of "conversion," in the sense that it provided people with a higher standard of living. But the illusion was short-lived. Locked in protected national economies it had no choice but to offer jobs, increase salaries and support social policies which in the end, turned against us by making us "consumers" who were indispensable for the creation of profits. The loans and investments to the exploited Third World countries were supposed to serve as the launching pad for their economies. But the masks soon fell and the noose tightened! The major corporations and western banks in the South, under the leadership of the World Bank and the IMF, forced these nations to open their borders, devaluate their currency, slash their social programs and dismantle their economy in order to re-finance the Third-World debt. The predators were then able to go in and help themselves to the labour pool and the local resources in order to use them for their own competitive advantage on the world market. At the same time they applied pressure on the governments of the North, demanding that they remove themselves as regulators of the economy and that they conclude international agreements allowing for the free circulation of capital, services and goods.

Once capital was freed of national constraints it began to undermine any previous social strides that had been made. This new structure is what we refer to today as neoliberalism where "the mar-

---

[3] Aboriginal Rights Coalition, *Aboriginal Perspectives on the Jubilee*, 3.

ket rules and the government manages."[4] Needless to say, it is the opposite of the true meaning of Jubilee.

The uncontrolled competition that resulted has created a situation where peoples, businesses and individuals are constantly at war with one another. The strongest eliminate the others. The race to get "more" or the search for competitiveness means that there will always be a race to give "less" for jobs, salaries,[5] working conditions, environmental protection, etc. This is a structure that serves to maintain large profits despite decreasing world demand.

And what are the workers told? That they must be "flexible" and "adapt" until they become "useless." The technology that was supposed to promote the well-being of all people is being used to exclude other competitors and to do away with the productive input of human work. Roving capital, in its ongoing search for maximum profitability, transforms shareholders into dictators who do not hesitate to force massive layoffs as the price of their remaining on board with the company. The profits generated by this system are "pumped" into financial markets that function in a sort of autonomous bubble made up of speculative transactions where "dormant" money begets money all the while removed from the production of real goods and services.

It is not surprising that we see an ever-increasing disparity of income in all societies. Wealth is becoming increasingly concentrated and privatised. The sources of this wealth, the *land*, especially in the rural areas of the Third World and jobs elsewhere, is no longer accessible to the people. How are they supposed to find the needed income to purchase even the most basic commodities? Statistics show that this degradation is happening all over the world. Between 1960 and 1991 the revenues of the wealthiest twenty percent of the world

---

[4] I. Ramonet, "Davos," *Le Monde Diplomatique*, March 1996, 1.

[5] In 1976 a person had to work 41 hours a week at minimum wage to cross over the threshold of poverty, today one has to work 73 hours a week. (N. Deslisle, "Un emploi ne met plus a l'abri de la pauvreté," *La Presse*, April 14, 1997, 3).

went from being 30 times to 61 times more than that of the poorest twenty percent. In the United States, 1% of the citizens now possess nearly 40% of the national wealth. In Canada between 1981 and 1994 the share of revenue of the wealthiest twenty percent went from being 19 to 24 times that of the poorest twenty percent. *"The average salary of the heads of the 100 largest Canadian corporations was 3.4 million dollars in 1998, an increase of 26% over the 2.7 million average they were paid in 1997. Meanwhile the profits of these same companies dropped by 18% (...) and countless employees were dismissed."*[6]

Redistribution turned upside down

Cornered by the financial markets they depend on for the financing of their debts and refuse to regulate, governments find themselves in a position where they have to accept the economic and social policies dictated by outside financial markets. Those who refuse to bow to this pressure see their financial rating drop and their debt increase. The redistribution of wealth by the State cannot correct the inequalities since the State pursues the same economic vision. The State, which is supposed to defend the common good, is really dealing a deadly blow to the poor and the middle classes by cutting assistance[7] and social services, and increasing income taxes in order to channel the gains to the wealthy by providing tax shelters, encouraging privatization and giving grants to businesses in return for their investments,[8] etc. After having done all of this, governments try to save face by making a big deal about handing out a few well-advertised grants here and there and by calling for social solidarity by the promotion of food banks, telethons, etc.! The business lobbies are 'sitting in the driver's seat' and are the ones drafting various Bills for the

---

[6] S. Truffaut, "Moi y'en a vouloir des sous," *Le Devoir*, May 11, 1999, 1.

[7] People on unemployment and on social assistance are thus obliged to take any job they can find. The State supplies employers with clusters of slaves disguised as citizens.

[8] According to *TIME* magazine, the U. S. government changed who would be the beneficiaries of "welfare" by giving $125 billion, the equivalent of the income tax paid by 60 million households, to businesses and large corporations that often cut more jobs than they created. (S Truffaut, "L'état stratégique, *Le Devoir*, November 6, 1998, 1). In Quebec recently, the Minister of Finance offered $350M to General Motors even before the company made a formal request for subsidies.

government, as confessed by John D. Rockefeller at the signing of the NAFTA agreement.[9] Nothing important is adopted by the federal government of Canada without first being approved by the Business Council of National Issues (BCNI) who often present the government with complete 'packages of analyses and recommendations' long before Ottawa issues its own discussion papers.[10]

Neoliberalism has truly gone too far and has lost all credibility. The people have had enough of the abuse. They are beginning to lift their heads in search of a clear call for a social agenda that will finally be in keeping with their aspirations. Neoliberalism can be dismantled, but a more just social order will not fall out of the blue. It can only come from a strong collective commitment rooted in hope.

The Jubilee: an ancient utopia to the rescue of modern society

The biblical tradition of the Jubilee can help free us from our yoke and get the world off to a new start. In the year 1250 before our era, Israel was born out of an alliance between those who fled from Egypt and the Hebrew peasants from Canaan who succeeded in gaining emancipation from the lords and the cities that held them hostage. The common experience of a God who liberates was, for this new society composed of tribes, clans and families, manifested in the equal distribution of land. One witnesses here the invention of a just social order. Later on inequalities surfaced once more when the people succumbed to the temptation of organizing themselves into kingdoms. Heavy taxes, abuse and forced labor again were imposed by the governing class made up of bureaucrats, merchants and large property owners. Injustice caused Israel to weaken, fall apart, and be sent into exile.

It is during this period of exile that the Jubilee legislation was written. Upon their return to the land, the Israelites' goal was once again to put into practice the vigilant solidarity of the old confedera-

---

[9] Tony Clark, Maude Barlow, *The Silent Coup, Confronting Big Business Takeover of Canada*, Ottawa and Toronto: CCPA and James Lorimer, 1997, 3.

[10] Ibid., 21-23.

tive organisation. In an agrarian society, the land was the main source of subsistence. It was a family's heirloom. Although they could dispose of the income and fruit of the land, the land itself could neither be purchased nor sold. Sometimes the family had to borrow money, or mortgage their products, or a piece or even all of their land due to a poor harvest or unjust pricing. This is where the second prescription came into play, since it provided for the correction of this situation by stipulating that every fifty years any acquired deeds or rights over another's property must be given back to them. Each family would once again have access to the ancestral land that had been allotted them to meet their needs. This "advanced" society knew that the only way to avoid the disintegration of their society was to regulate the rules of the market game. Fatalism had no place in the order of things.

The Jubilee redistribution of wealth: A requirement of our faith in God

Another scriptural text that summarizes all of these Jubilee prescriptions is *"let there be no poor among you"* (Dt. 15.4). This is the "charter of Israel," an imperative that flowed from their experience of God and that called upon their social creativity. The foundation of Israel rested on two main events; the *liberation from slavery* in Egypt by breaking away from the Pharaonic order, and the *granting of land* which would allow all to meet their needs. The children of Israel never forgot that the land belonged to God and that they would only ever be *strangers and guests* (Lev. 25.23) in that place. This made it literally impossible for the powerful to take over the land and to prey on the vulnerable. They knew that their Covenant community would be destroyed if they allowed economic laws alone to dominate their lives. It would be as if God's person were being attacked and as if they had *returned to Egypt*. The Jubilee is therefore a *break from*, rooted in the priority of the logic of *gift* upon which Israel is founded. Israel is well aware of its indebtedness to God where each person can accede to that which is rightfully theirs and gives them the right to share equally in the *common riches* of God's realm. Recognition of Yahweh's exclusive sovereignty freed the people of any false absolutes that would destroy the community and allowed the members to take responsibility for one another and for their common future.

Although the Israelites probably rarely implemented the Jubilee prescriptions, they never really lost sight of them. The prophets condemned the accumulation of houses and fields (Mi. 2.2), the holding back of vital security pledges for the debtors (Am. 2.8) and the fraudulent exploitation of the poor (Am. 8.4-6). Isaiah spoke of a "new earth," a place where one could build a house and plant a vineyard for ones own family and not have to hand over all the profits to the owner, a place where the wolf and the young lamb would feed together (Is. 65.17-25). Jesus linked his mission to the *Lord's year of favor,* or in other words, the Jubilee (Lk. 4.19). This is "Good News for the poor" but "bad news" for the rich urbanites who have coveted the land of the peasants because they were unable to pay excessive taxes. The re-distribution of wealth is at the heart of these positions. One may recall: the multiplication of the bread (the direct result of sharing); or the call addressed to the rich young man (Mk. 10. 17-31); or Zacchaeus, who offers to give half of everything he owns to the poor and somehow return a portion of that which he had wrongfully taken from them (Lk. 19.1-10); or the workers of the eleventh hour who had the same rights as the others to have what they needed to live; or the first Christians who were moved to share their possessions with those facing want *"so that each one would have what they needed."* (Acts 2, 44-47); or finally the doctrine of the universal destination of goods, whereby the Fathers of the Church in the fourth century gave the *koinonia* (i.e., social solidarity) precedence over property.

To live the Jubilee is to dream of another kind of society in spite of the exile imposed upon us by neoliberalism

What meaning does the Jubilee hold for us today? It certainly flies in the face of any attempts on the part of the market and the neo-liberal state to convince us that "we really don't have a choice" and that we must submit to the economic rules as they exist today. It forbids having to sacrifice people on the losing end and society itself in the name of those same rules. The market is not God and it must never be given priority over the needs and the dignity of persons. The Jubilee authorizes us to hope and to dream of a society where everyone would have their rightful place. It reminds us that it is the people and not the market that should be setting the social agenda. It highlights the fact that humanity owes nothing to anything except to itself and especially to God, and God does not ask for anything for God's person. All God wants is for us to be concerned about the fate of the poor and the little ones, to speak for those who "don't count" and who are refused access to even a small part of the "common good" (Math. 25).

God calls the Church to be counter-cultural, to be *ecclesia*, which was the name the Israelites gave to the assembly made up of the egalitarian confederation of tribes, in other words to provide an alternative to society as we know it today. What an enormous challenge! God models this for us in the way each one of us is asked to live the Eucharist. Here God uses 'economic' products such as bread and wine—fruit of the work of human hands—to reveal the Godhead and to be present with us. God similarly asks that our economic life together in society be a sign of God's paternal and maternal presence, that we make of the economy a "sacrament." In order for this to happen the economy must be organised in accordance with the logic of gratuitousness and gift, for this is the only basis upon which we can found the 'common reasons' of our living together. This logic already exists and is revealed to us by the "Spirit who renews the face of the earth." Will we be able to recognise the presence of the Spirit in the initiatives that await our active support within our own milieu?

Translation from French by Patricia Leahy.

Michel Beaudin, is a professor at the Faculty of Theology, University of Montréal.

2

Jubilee Revisited: A Reflection[1]

Paul E. Hansen C.Ss.R.

The Churches in Canada along with other groups have come upon the biblical theme of Jubilee as a way of animating their faith life and re-animating some of the work of the Canadian Church Coalitions that, since the early seventies, have been deeply concerned about a faith that does justice. This effort of the Canadian Churches has gained a worldwide recognition and appreciation. Having worked in Rome for the past seven years and having visited all continents, I heard of the work of the Canadian Churches and being a Canadian, often shared in words and gestures of gratitude. The Canadian Ecumenical Church Coalitions were and are a way of being about a socially committed faith, unique in our world. They are a special moment for many peoples, sister churches, faith communities and those struggling for justice and peace around the world.

Having returned to Canada from living in a "new" Europe, I note that things have dramatically changed in many areas of societal life here. For example, at a meeting of Church leaders and politicians it was a believer, not **an official church** leader who gave the theological reflection that began our day. Her presentation was prophetic, insightful and awe-inspiring. In the following weeks, I wondered if **church officialdom** had much to say in and to this new emerging societal reality. I did find in JUBILEE a creative attempt.

As Judeo-Christians we are living in millennial times. Our context is not clear. A way forward is not immediately obvious. Biblical Jubilee offers an insight that may guide and give an important text to this our context.

---

[1] The reflections and insights for this reflection paper originated in conversations following a retreat given in Rome in 1996 to SEDOS by Carlos Mesters, a Dutch Carmelite theologian working in Brazil and a presentation by J.L. Ska of the Biblicum in the Fall of 1998 to the Commission for Justice, Peace and the Integrity of Creation of the Union of Superiors General. It is also the result of conversations over the past summer (1999) especially with Jo Nazar.

Jubilee inspiration most probably arose during and out of the Babylonian Captivity, a time of exile, a time of uncertainty, a time of yearning and anticipation, in a way much like our own times. Like the times of exile, these post-modern times point to a diversity of opinions concerning the nature of reality and how life is to be lived, celebrated, cared for and shared.

Jubilee inspiration arising out of the Babylonian Exile has its clearest expression in Leviticus 25. For us Judeo-Christians however, Luke 4 quoting Isaiah 61 (a text also arising out of the Babylonian captivity) calls us to an even clearer expression of the Jubilee message and vocation. However, this message and vocation is clothed in garments of Light and Shadow.

Biblical Jubilee

The biblical reality of Jubilee is a multi-faceted image, symbol and metaphor. As first expressed in Leviticus 25, it speaks of debt release, freeing of slaves, distribution of wealth, care and love of the land. It invites an **economics of enough** and justice toward one another and the land. This inspiration and vocation is found in the Torah—the first five books of the Jewish scriptures. Rabbis suggest that this inspiration of the Torah is a "being existing before the creation of the world as the will of God." The **vocation and task** of Jubilee was to be the attitude and the disposition of the Tribes of Yahweh as they entered the Land of Canaan, the Promised Land.

However this **people of God** entering the promised land is not as simple and clear as the movie *The Ten Commandments* might have us believe. At this point in scholarship and research there is no consensus on the issue of the origin of the Israelites. It seems that Israel came to be in the land of Canaan as a result of many socio-political forces and movements of peoples. There are traces of a slave revolt in Egypt but no clear record of it. There are traces of a peasant revolt in the land of Canaan along with bands of Robin Hood type folks fighting for their rights. It seems that various movements and groups came together to found what we call today the People of God or the Israelites (McDermot, *What are They Saying about the Formation of Israel?*)

During the Babylonian Captivity the various written fragments, stories, oral traditions, myths, inspirations and foundational and formative events were probably given their format and became the primary narrative of the scriptures. As Walter Brueggemann suggests: "This is the most important story we know and we have come to believe it is decisively about us."*(The Bible Makes Sense, 46.)* Israel's primary narrative can be located in three texts. It is the story a community relies upon in crisis and the one by which the truth or falseness of every other story is judged. (Deut. 26:5-9; Deut. 6:20-24; Josh. 24:1-13). Deuteronomy 26: 5-9 states:

> A wandering Aramean was my ancestor; he went down into Egypt and lived there as an alien, few in numbers, and there became a great nation, might and populous. When the Egyptians treated us harshly and afflicted us, we cried to the Lord, the God of our ancestors; the Lord heard our voice and saw our affliction, out toil and oppression. The Lord brought us out of Egypt with a mighty hand and an outstretched arm, with a terrifying display of power and with signs and wonders and brought us into this place and gave us this land, a land flowing with milk and honey.

Judges and Kings

Norman Gottwald and others suggest that one of the reasons the Israelites became the people of God or **a light to the nations** was because they attempted a society without Kings, one built on an attempt at socialism led by Judges who strived for equality and caring among the Tribes. This history was short lived. Primarily due to needs for defense and protection and along with a desire for a tighter political reality the **peoples** called upon the need for a King. Hence the choice and call of Saul, David and Solomon, to name the first three. This is crucial to appreciate in terms of having a sense of the Bible as a primary narrative and source of inspiration for our life today.

It was under the Kings and especially Solomon that an **economics of satiation** was created within Israel. The Solomonic achievement was one of incredible well-being and affluence (1Kings 4: 20-23). It is difficult to keep a revolution of freedom and justice under way when there is satiation. The high standard of living claimed by the text is fully supported by the archaeology of the period (Brueggemann). Covenant-ing, which takes brothers and sisters seriously had been replaced by consuming which regards brothers and sisters as products to be used (*Royal Consciousness*).

It was shortly thereafter that the prophets within Israel were called forth by God to remind the people of the covenant and their early inspiration as a people. We have now the beginning of what I would call a tension between Royal Consciousness and Prophetic Consciousness right up to and including the return from the Babylonian Captivity and the building of the Second Temple. Royal Consciousness is the per-spective seen by the Kings and the Temple Leaders within Israel while the Prophetic Consciousness is that of the prophets who are called by God to remind the people of the covenant and hence God's will for them. Both realities are to be found in the scriptures. (It should be noted that both Royal and Prophetic Consciousness are not cut and dried categories of understanding but rather are useful insights in appre-ciating the light and shadow sides of Jubilee). The insight and inspira-tion of Jubilee has to be seen in this context, in this tension, if we are to do justice to the scriptures and if we are to know the role of the Word of God in the discernment of what our faith life lived might be today. To say it in the words of Jesse Jackson: "every text without a context is a pretext."

Context of Jubilee

To appreciate a theological reflection around Jubilee one must see two major events in the life of the people of God coming together:

1) Leviticus of the first Exodus from Egypt;
2) The building of the Second Temple arising out of the Second Exodus from the Babylonian Captivity.

We have a Jubilee theology in both events and probably—since the writing down was during the captivity and shortly thereafter—more influenced by the Second Exodus from the Babylonian Captivity. In other words the real context of Jubilee is not Leviticus and entering the Promised Land but rather that of Cyrus freeing the Israelites from captivity and their going **home** to build the Temple anew. This action provides a shadow side to Jubilee. While the Prophetic Consciousness of Jubilee leads to inspiration and gratitude, the Royal Consciousness concerns of Jubilee—militarism, taking of the lands, forced labour—leads to oppression for some. We living today have to own and see this in our work and faith life. If we are to use the scriptural notion of Jubilee then we cannot use it in a literal way. We must see Jubilee as an inspiration so very valid for our times but having a complicated history of light and shadow.

The year of Jubilee or Holy Year, which is celebrated every fifty years, is indeed a festivity of biblical origin. Maria Harris in her work: *Proclaim Jubilee* suggests that justice is the core theme of Jubilee. Justice is a steady way of being in the world and being of God. "To know God is to do justice" proclaimed the prophet Jeremiah. Harris suggests that Jubilee justice is an alternative way of living given the present order of things.

There is an important principle which never should be forgotten when the Bible is being read, especially the Jewish Scriptures: it is better not to look for immediate answers to our questions and ready solutions to our problems. The Bible speaks to questions and problems, which occurred in those days when the books it contains were written. To understand the biblical message it is important to see how the biblical authors sought to resolve problems, which occurred in their time, so that in turn, we may find adequate answers to similar problems that occur today.

As for all the laws, the ones on Jubilee spoke to specific questions. Why then are the laws of Lev. 25 asking to leave fields unploughed, to give back land and houses to their original owners, to redeem slaves and financially help the needy? Biblical society, not unlike the so-called **Third World** of today, was mainly composed of persons who struggled for life. Some go as far as saying that in those days 90% of the population were living under the poverty line (J.L. Ska, Pontifical Biblical Institute). People were lucky in those days if they were not dying of hunger or illness. Very little was needed to project a family into deep misery: a bad harvest, drought, disease of cattle, war, a too sudden upset on some debt, could all have immediate and catastrophic consequences. Food was bought and money borrowed at high cost in order to survive. To be able to purchase meant often going into debt. In order to pay debts, one had to sell one's few belongings: house, freedom and in this latter case it meant that your children and yourself were sold as slaves. Only the rich and powerful had in fact the necessary means to face such difficult hardships as starvation. At a certain point there are so many poor and sick people that the situation becomes unbearable and threatens to explode. There is a need for a reaction. This is how laws similar to the ones of biblical Jubilee come about. This was not unique to Israel, other ancient civilisations reacted in such fashion.

Reference to Jubilee in the Jewish Scriptures is quite rare. Other than Leviticus 25 we only have three other sources of any magnitude. The Book of Ezekiel is the only one that clearly mentions a law concerning the reconstruction of Israel during the remission year (Ez. 46:17; cf Lev. 25:10). But the prophet's text does not get specific where redeeming slaves takes place.

Jeremiah 34 describes a collective remission of slaves and servants, which was decided by King Sedecias shortly before Jerusalem's fall. However good intentions did not last long. The owners changed their minds quickly enough to again enslave their previous servants. Moreover the Law called upon is not that of Lev. 25, the Jubilee Law, but that of Deut. 15, one of the laws of the sabbatical year, which required the redeeming of those who had become slaves because of the debt in the seventh year.

Nehemiah 5 also gives an example. The Governor of Judea, the King of Persia's envoy, faced a major problem in Israel. Most of the population was in debt. Father and Mothers complained to Nehemiah that they have to reduce their children to slavery or pledge their fields and vineyards. Nehemiah proposes a radical solution: cancellation of debts: "Restitute without any delay, fields, vineyards, olive trees and houses and cancel the loan that has been granted, be it money, corn, wine or oil." This decision recalls Deut. 15, which states literally the cancellation of debt. But no mention is made of Jubilee or a celebration. Nehemiah 10:32 is another text which connects to the sabbatical year, but not to the year of Jubilee: "We shall let go of the earth's products during the seventh year, as well as of all debts."

Have Jubilee Laws Ever Been Applied?

We have to bow to the fact that there is no formal proof in the Jewish Scriptures that the Holy Year of Jubilee had ever been celebrated. Those who claim that the Jubilee year was followed must claim so on probabilities, not on facts.

Why was the Law of Jubilee probably not put into force? The reasons are many. Fifty years is a long time, which was above the life expectancy of most people of this era, especially the poor. If someone became a slave right after a Jubilee year, he/she had not much chance to be redeemed before his/her death. It must also be considered that to put a freeing of slaves, debt and the giving back of lands into practice would have created probably chaos, a complex situation difficult to control.

The most interesting theory in this matter and the one that I would support considers the Jubilee celebrations as a remembrance of the end of Exodus or Exile in the Babylonian Captivity. The exile in Babylon lasted about 50 years from 586-536 BCE. The end of the exile was welcomed as a liberation. God has redeemed the people from slavery in Babylon as God had also redeemed Israel from Egypt (Jr. 16: 14-25; 25:7-8, Isaiah 40:2). God also restituted to the people their lands and houses. Maybe Leviticus laws wanted to perpetuate this remembrance and introduce a festivity, which could remember this event. There probably is more involved. When exiles started to return they must have found their lands and houses occupied by those who had stayed in the country. When an invading army conquered another people often the poor and the peasants were left behind and the leaders, the rich and the artisans were taken into captivity and exile. Maybe the law would represent an appeal to restitute to their first owners what they owned before Jerusalem's fall and one could even imagine that they got them back (note East Germany and other parts of Eastern Europe etc. today). Maybe that is why Jesus, the Galilean coming from the Galilee, the "Land of the Nations," was not always excited about the goings on in Jerusalem and why he sided with the poor, marginalized and those abused by power and debt. However, this whole subject remains very conjectural.

What Was Going On In Jerusalem Around 536 BCE?

To help us come to a very important word of encouragement which invites us to work for and take inspiration from the reality of Jubilee, let us re-capture the prophetic vocation within Israel. We need to keep this in mind if we want to have a way forward. As we all know the work of the prophet Isaiah is divided into three parts. First Isaiah deals with the time before the Babylonian Captivity. Second Isaiah deals with the time spent in captivity. Third Isaiah deals with the desire for and the return to Jerusalem, the eventual building of the Second Temple and the end of the Exile in Babylon. For those of us who are Christian and attempt to follow the Way of the person Jesus, it is important that we know Isaiah. Maybe Isaiah 61 and this text read as Luke 4 by Jesus in the synagogue at Nazareth are the most important texts in the scriptures in terms of inspiration and calling as we attempt to be Jubilee People in these our times. Our calling upon Leviticus 25 is important but must be filtered and lived through Isaiah 61 and repeated in Luke 4.

First Isaiah sees the people of God suffering in exile because they have disobeyed and deserve to be punished. Second Isaiah sees the peoples' suffering as a purification that they might see anew, the new deed being done and Third Isaiah sees the peoples' suffering as a preparation or a vocation to be **a light to the nations.** Isaiah tells the people that it is no longer necessary to recall the past, can they not see the new deed that is being done (Is. 43). Cyrus, who initiated the Second Exodus—the new deed being done—is in a sense, replacing Moses of the First Exodus (Is. 44 and 45). Cyrus the pagan from Persia is referred to by Isaiah as "he is my shepherd" (Is. 44) a title that was used only for King David. Carlos Mesters likes to note that for the Israelites to hear that Cyrus was the **Shepherd** and the author of the upcoming liberation from captivity would be like Ronald Reagan seeing a leader of the Soviet Union as the saviour of the world. Psychologically speaking this is hard for many to see and accept. To do so would mean a whole new way of thinking and conceptualizing the working of God in history and so many people remained in Babylon and did not go back to Jerusalem.

End of Exile and Building of the Second Temple

It is accepted by scholars that the Exile in Babylon lasted about 50 years. Jubilee was to be celebrated in the 50th year. One can see the possible connection.

The fall of Babylon to the Persians signalled a new era for the people of Yahweh. Beginning with Cyrus the "anointed one" (Is. 45) and later Persian rulers, the empire sought a strong military and loyal presence particularly near the trouble spots, in this case Egypt. Hence, the sending back to Jerusalem people who would be loyal and who would help fulfil this imperial necessity. Cyrus did not only seek to liberate the Israelites but others who were captured and held in Babylon as well (Cyrus Cylinder, 538). The resumption of the temple states was essential to the stability of the empire. Temples in antiquity were not only centres of worship. They were very much the centre of the entire life of the people. Temples were for ancient civilisations, the centre of politics, commerce, religion and social life. Harvests and weapons were stored there. Economic development depended on the Temple. Indeed, there existed a symbiotic relationship between the city-state and the temple state. From these various temple states Persian rulers were able to collect the royal tributes or taxes to finance the rule and expansion of the empire. This policy was given great impetus by Darius I who continued the work begun by Cyrus.

Since this return and possible implementation of the Laws of Jubilee are seen as part of Cyrus-Darius' military expansion and consolidation, then the returning of lands and houses is an oppression and a subjugation of peoples on the land who did not go into exile. In this context then the building of the Second Temple must be seen as an oppression for the poor and the peasant population. This is the shadow side of Jubilee, the perspective of Royal Consciousness. As Walter Brueggemann suggests in his work: *Prophetic Imagination,* in order to come to a sense of the message called Revelation, or the Word of God, one must see insights or teachings like Leviticus 25 for example in the context of this tension between Royal and Prophetic Consciousness. While Jubilee laws are probably to be seen as an application of the return from Exile in Babylon and the building of the Second Temple and an oppression for some, nevertheless we today can draw inspiration from Jubilee by recalling Jubilee's roots in prophetic imagination as well as that of royal consciousness. We do a dis-service to the Word of God in a literal reading or in a reading that dismisses the context of these times.

Luke 4, Isaiah 61: True Jubilee Inspiration

It sees to me to be very important for us who are doing work as the Canadian Ecumenical Jubilee Initiative to bring into reflection not only the Leviticus text and the texts relating to the building of the Second Temple and the return from exile in Babylon but also the vocation expressed by Jesus as he entered the synagogue of Nazareth in Luke 4, took up the scroll of the Prophet Isaiah and read:

> The spirit of the Lord God is upon me, because the Lord has anointed me; he has sent me to bring good news to the op-pressed, to bind up the brokenhearted, to proclaim liberty to the captives, and release to the prisoners; to proclaim the year of the Lord's favour (Isaiah 61, Luke 4).

I am of the conviction that while recognizing Leviticus 25 as a dream of Jubilee and a re-animation of faith life, nevertheless the inspiration of Isaiah and the vocation of Jesus as expressed in Luke 4 are more important and have an easier application to a faith that does justice in our context today than does Leviticus 25. People who want to live out of the Jewish-Christian tradition must see these two texts as crucial to Jubilee work for they are the heart of the Prophetic Consciousness and they are the call to a life of discipleship. While the primary narrative of the scriptures is foundational in our faith life, we nevertheless live in the presence of a living God in these our times. While in one sense the scriptures could be seen to be normative, on the other hand, the scriptures must be placed in a dialogue with the signs of these living times, for "every text without a context is a pretext."

These times cry out for Jubilee inspiration. The Third World debt is killing millions of our brothers and sisters, especially in Africa and parts of Latin America. Many are becoming slaves to a globalization of the economy. Destruction of the land on our planet earth is increasing and there is a new cry for wealth distribution. To be people of God we must say with our lives NO to this destruction and death. The important concern for us today is to BE Jesus for these our times as it is to know him. What does it mean to BE Jesus for these our times? I would suggest attitudes of being Jesus today might be found in the biblical BEATITUDES which find their first inspiration in the prophet Isaiah especially Isaiah 61. It is this inspiration that Jesus read out to the elders and the people in the synagogue of Nazareth recorded in Luke 4. This is the vocation that we are to consider as our calling in Jubilee prayer, reflection and work.

As people of faith, let us continue in discipleship. Let us continue to live and proclaim Jubilee personally, collectively, prophetically and socio-politically in these our times. In doing so let us never forget that we too live in the tension of Royal and Prophetic Consciousness in both their Light and Shadow.

Paul Hansen is a member of the Redemptorist Order and the director of his Order's Biblical Justice Advocacy/Consultancy in English Canada. Paul recently returned to Canada from Rome where, for six years, he was the Director of the General Secretariat for Justice, Peace and the Integrity of Creation for the Redemptorists. In that capacity he visited his Order worldwide receiving a first hand awareness of the plight of millions marginal to power and the destruction of our eco-system.

Bibliography

Brueggemann, Walter (1991). *Abiding Astonishment.* Kentucky: Westminister/John Knox Press.

Brueggemann, Walter (1983). *The Bible Makes Sense.* Winona, MN: St. Mary's Press.

Brueggemann, Walter (1989). *Finally Comes The Poet.* Minneapolis, Augsburg Fortress.

Brueggemann, Walter (1986). *Hopeful Imagination.* Philadelphia: Fortress Press.

Brueggemann, Walter (1983). *Prophetic Imagination.* Philadelphia: Fortress Press.

Davies, Philip R. ed. (1991). *Second Temple Studies 1 Persian Period.* JSOT

             (1994). *Second Temple Studies 2 Temple Community in the Persian Period.* JSOT. (Sheffield: Sheffield Academic Press).

Gottwald, Norman (1981). *Tribes Of Yahweh.* Maryknoll: Orbis Press.

Gottwald, Norman (1985). *The Hebrew Bible.* Philadelphia: Fortress Press.

Harris, Maria (1996). *Proclaim Jubilee.* Kentucky: Westminister/ John Knox Press.

McDermott, John J. (1998*). What Are They Saying About—The Formation of Israel?* New York, Paulist Press.

Mesters, Carlos (1996) Notes given at a Retreat to SEDOS, Rome.

Meyers, Carol L., Meyers, Eric M. (1987*). The Anchor Bible—Haggai, Zechariah 1-8.* New York: Doubleday.

Peterson, David (1984). *The Old Testament Library—Haggai and Zechariah,* 1-8. Philadelphia: Westminister Press.

Ska, J.L. (1998). *A Few Remarks On The Year Of Jubilee—Biblical Founda-tion.* A conference given to the Commission for Justice, Peace and the Integrity of Creation of the Union of Superiors General Rome.

3

Jubilee in the New Testament

Maria Theresa Porcile Santiso

The Gospel of Jesus according to Luke

There is no evidence in the history of the people of Israel that Jubilee—literally—as such, ever existed. So it is valid to ask ourselves: Is it a utopia? Is it an idealistic "vision" that arose in the period of exile? If we go to Luke's Gospel with that question will we be able to find an echo in the message of Jesus?

When we compare the initial references to Jesus' public life in the synoptic gospels we find that there are aspects of them which distinguish each of these visions from the others. What is the peculiar quality of Luke? This emerges in part through a reading of the other Gospels. In Mark we read:

> Now after John was arrested, Jesus came to Galilee, proclaiming the good news of God, and saying, 'The time is fulfilled and the kingdom of God has come near; repent, and believe in the good news (Mark 1:14-15).

According to Matthew, Jesus was in Galilee (4:12) and began to preach, saying:

> Repent, for the kingdom of heaven has come near (Matthew 4:17).

It is typical that Luke places the preaching of Jesus in the Jewish liturgical framework of the synagogue of Nazareth where, as it says in the text, Jesus began "as was his custom (Luke 4:16)." Jesus read there the passage from the prophet Isaiah (61:1-2). In accordance with the practice of that synagogue, he was given the scroll, opened it and "found." That is to say, he found the passage which he wished to read. When he finished reading he said: "TODAY this scripture has been fulfilled (Lk 4:21)."

The verb "fulfil" appears in Mark 1:15 and several times in Luke's Gospel of Jesus as well as in the Gospel of the Spirit, the Acts of the Apostles, and the Infancy Gospel of Luke (1:21, 23, 45 and 2:6, 21, 22). It is central to the relationship between the theology of promise and the theology of time. The new element is that now Jesus is saying "TODAY."

What is to be the relationship between the "kingdom of heaven at hand" which Matthew and Mark mention and the TODAY "fulfilling" the prophecy of Isaiah which culminates in the year of grace?

A reading of Luke using the interpretive framework of "the Jubilee-Kingdom perspective" opens up a horizon of unsuspected understanding. Luke 4:21 has been written about copiously, especially in Latin America and in the context of a vision of liberation. The extraordinary thing we discover is that a whole chain of (references to) "TODAY" exists in Luke, the Gospel of Jesus, as well as in the Gospel of the Spirit, the Acts of the Apostles.

The TODAY of the synagogue in Nazareth has another resonance when it is seen as part of this chain of twelve "Todays" which will appear throughout the Gospel. Eleven of them are found in the accounts of Jesus' public ministry and one in the "Infancy Narratives"

The Today of Impossible Liberation (Luke 19:1-10)

If we had been thinking that the TODAY of salvation in the Synagogue was only for those who were considered poor, understood as those who were victims of the tribute system of Imperial Rome, that is to say, if we had been thinking of the oppressed in the material, economic and cultural sense, the passage which follows is going to surprise us.

What are the foreshadowings of this episode? It is helpful to review the Lucan Gospel to this point, to re-read several earlier actions and teachings of Jesus, in order to understand the Zacchaeus passage.

Let us review quickly some of these key texts which allow us to gain a better perspective and understanding of the pericope of Zacchaeus. All of these texts place us in situations of social, cultural and personal conflicts and contrasts: the bent-over woman, Dives and Lazarus, the pharisee and the tax collector, the rich young man, the blind man in Jericho.

It would seem that Luke has been preparing the reader for the surprising incident involving Zacchaeus. In earlier chapters he has presented encounters or occasions in which seemingly random elements appear which later will come together in the events in which Zacchaeus is the main character.

Luke has made us think about the action of Jesus in healing a bent-over woman, a "daughter of Abraham," on the Sabbath, the day of liberation (Luke 13:17):

> When he said this, all his adversaries were covered in confusion, and all the people were overjoyed at all the wonders he worked (Luke 13:17; cf Luke 1:14, 4:15).

As on other occasions, it is shown that everyone is seduced by the actions of Jesus, that these wonders cause them to rejoice (cf Luke 5:26, 7:16-17). For our reading here it is significant that the identity of the woman as a "daughter of Abraham" is restored, as will happen with Zacchaeus.

Further on we encounter the dramatic and very contemporary story of the "rich man" (whose name we do not know), who "feasted magnificently every day (Luke 16:19)," and apparently didn't even see Lazarus, the poor man covered with sores lying at his gate, who "longed to fill himself with the scraps that fell from the rich man's table" (verse 21), until they both died and the rich man, now in Hell, looked up and saw Lazarus in the bosom of Abraham (Luke 16:23).

For our reading we note the way Luke presents this rich man, as both indifferent and nameless. What Luke will say in the pericope of Zacchaeus will show the importance that the gospel writer places not only on the possibility of "conversion," but also on the position that person holds, in an intimate encounter as between friends.

Next we encounter the parable of the Pharisee and the tax collector. There they are, the Pharisee, who feels he has every right to pray, and the tax collector who stands far off and doesn't even dare to raise his eyes to heaven (Luke 18:14).

The contrast is clear between the first man, who has given himself to studying and following the law and is a normative symbol of faith and morality in his society, and the second man, at the lowest level in the Jewish social structure and farthest away from the religious and ethical precepts of the nation.

Luke puts these words in the mouth of the Pharisee, who "stood there" and prayed, saying: 'I thank you, God, that I am not thieving, unjust, adulterous like the rest of mankind, and particularly that I am not like this tax collector. I fast twice a week; I pay tithes on all I get.' (Luke

18:11).'" This is contrasted with the publican who says: "Oh God, be merciful to me, a sinner (Luke 18:13)."

How many times do we hear or say things like this? We give thanks for the families in which we were raised, for the good education we have received, for the opportunities we have had. Of course that is a reason to be thankful, but if all that is not converted into responsibility, which comes out of the word "response and is not translated into service to others out of humble love, then this is **a reversal of what the kingdom requires of us**. We have but to recall the parable of the talents (Matthew 25:10ff, cf Luke 16:9-13).

Further along in the account of Jesus' travels there appears the dialogue with the rich man seeking perfection What is clear is that this has to do with a rich man who has kept the commandments since his youth (Luke 18:21) and now is looking for "eternal life." Faced with the response from Jesus, this appears to him to be impossible, and the rich man leaves, rich and sad (Luke 18:18-27).

This is presented as "fatalism," impotence, slavery, "inability" to change, a lack of freedom, a paralyzing condition which comes out of his wealth. For this rich man, who really is searching, it is "impossible" to give up his wealth. He doesn't even pause to think over Jesus' response. It is impossible for him to stop being rich, to change the direction of his life. And so he is left with his search and his fatal sadness.

Even so, he did take the initiative to ask Jesus. What had caused him to do this? Could it have been curiosity? Could he have begun to be concerned that his sense of himself was being drowned by worries over "being an owner?" So many unnecessary worries, which drowned his deeper thirst.

We need to bear in mind this incident precedes Zacchaeus, in which it was impossible for a rich man to let go of his riches. Next, the text which immediately precedes the incident with Zacchaeus is the incident of the blind man in Jericho:

> Now as he drew near to Jericho there was a blind man sitting at the side of the road begging. When he heard the crowd going past he asked what it was all about, and they told him that Jesus the Nazarene was passing by. So he called out, 'Jesus, Son of David, have pity on me!' The people in front scolded him and told him to

keep quiet, but he shouted all the louder, 'Son of David, have pity on me!' Jesus stopped and ordered them to bring the man to him, and when he came, asked him, 'What do you want me to do for you?' 'Sir,' he replied, 'let me see again.' Jesus said to him, 'Receive your sight. Your faith has saved you.' And instantly his sight returned and he followed him praising God, and all the people who saw it gave praise to God for what had happened (Luke 18).

The blind man has the same cry as the tax collector in the parable (Luke 18:13). From Luke's point of view it is not happenstance that the incident with the blind man on the road to Jericho immediately precedes the incident with Zacchaeus in the city of Jericho. It is a matter of two sorts of blindness, one physical and the other spiritual.

The blind man could not see and cried out in faith. Neither could Zaccheus see (the proof of this is that he wanted to see, cf Luke 19:3); he also cried out internally, a secret cry which was not heard by the crowd who surrounded and rebuked him. It was heard by Jesus. He saw with some difficulty because of his short stature. But his interior attitude was "to be anxious to see" (cf Luke 19:3). We remember that blindness appears in the passage where Jesus reads from Isaiah 61 in the synagogue at Nazareth (Luke 4:18). Now Jesus is confronted by two types of blindness, and both are cured:

> He entered Jericho and was going through the town when a man whose name was Zacchaeus made his appearance; he was one of the senior tax collectors and a wealthy man. He was anxious to see what kind of man Jesus was, but he was too short and could not see him for the crowd; so he ran ahead and climbed a sycamore tree to catch a glimpse of Jesus who was to pass that way. When Jesus reached the spot he looked up and spoke to him: 'Zacchaeus, come down. Hurry, because I must stay at your house **TODAY**.' And he hurried down and welcomed him joyfully. They all complained when they saw what was happening. 'He has gone to stay at a sinner's house' they said. But Zacchaeus stood his ground and said to the Lord, 'Look, *sir*, I am going to give half my property to the poor, and if I have cheated anybody I will pay him back four times the amount.' And Jesus said to him, '**TODAY** salvation has come to this house, because this man too is a son of

Abraham. For the Son of Man has come **to seek out and save** what was lost' (Luke 19:1-10).' "

If we read this text as the echo of the TODAY in the Synagogue, there is an extraordinary surprise. There Jesus says **"TODAY** this scripture has been fulfilled (Luke 4:21)." Now he says of Zacchaeus, **"TODAY** salvation has come to this house because this man too is a son of Abraham (Luke 19:9)." What was announced in Nazareth is fully realized in Jericho.

The Zacchaeus text is fundamental in the context of the proclamation of the year of grace, the year of Jubilee. Zacchaeus opened his eyes and saw. Jesus continues to proclaim TODAY, but now the context is not public or liturgical; it is domestic, private. We imagine him in the situation of a personal encounter in a rich man's home which is likely quite magnificent. He who is called Master goes to the house of a man who is scorned (Luke 18:11), the object of complaints by those who believed themselves to be faithful to the Law.

But Zacchaeus is the truly pure, honest, upright one (and that is what his name means in Hebrew) and he **wanted** (as did Lazarus the beggar in Luke 16) to see Jesus; his "rich man's table" was the face of Jesus. The attitude of Zacchaeus is of one who is aware that he does not see, one who knows that in some area of his life he is needy, he is poor, he is blind. Jesus "looks up at him", as the text says (verse 5). And he pronounces the **TODAY**, responding fully to the desire of Zacchaeus. He will not only allow himself to be seen by him, he will stay in his home as well, with all that that signifies of intimacy, welcome and reciprocity of trust. And Zacchaeus receives him, in the face of the scandal and complaining it causes among the townsfolk.

Zacchaeus is rocked to the depths of his being by this attitude of Jesus, and he responds with a radical change of conduct. It is a manifest conversion. And something unexpected happens: He fulfills, as no one before has done, the words Jesus proclaimed in the Synagogue at Nazareth, the teaching about Sabbath and Jubilee. Zacchaeus is the liberated blind man who lives out the year of grace, and he does so abundantly. He gives away half of his possessions, and not only forgives debts but does much more; he gives back four times the amount he has stolen. He divests himself of what he has acquired through his unfair dealings, and he does so in a manner that makes him odious to the townspeople: He feels that he must make amends.

What has happened? When Jesus came to the tree where Zacchaeus was he looked into his heart. Jesus lifted his eyes, the same gesture he made with the disciples in the Beatitudes (Luke 6:20). He knew how to see in that despised man a potential disciple, as he was able to Matthew, when his gaze transformed him from a tax collector into a follower and evangelist (Luke 5:2-8).

Jesus sees in him the best quality his heart contains: his desire to see. Zacchaeus divests himself of his ill-gotten gains. Luke does not tell us even one word that Jesus could have said in private to Zacchaeus. There is no exhortation to conversion on Jesus' part, no discourse on "social justice," nothing. Zacchaeus simply does not resist the eyes of Jesus which look into the depths of his soul.

Zacchaeus had needed to allow himself to look freely, without fear, without hiding that which he was ashamed for Jesus to see: he wants to divest himself of what he has acquired. In Jesus there was certainly no reproach, no judgement, no prejudice, no irony, no scorn. Instead we too are able to hear with our hearts what he said with a look, saying with his eyes: "Zacchaeus...have trust do not worry...you wanted to see me...I give to you as one of my flock the Kingdom of my Father. You have worked so hard to enrich yourself; now abandon enrichment for the freedom of poverty, for the security of uncontrolled love. Look at the birds of the air..."

Jesus loved him, went to meet him without judging, lifted his eyes, stayed with him, welcomed his desire. Jesus knew his thoughts (Luke 5:22, 16:15). That is what happened: in a person-to-person relationship, Jesus sees the secret heart of the unchangeable person, beyond the social function which he held which was so criticized and hated. Jesus saw much more than the corruption of the role Zacchaeus had as a social exploiter, a sell-out to the empire and its imperialism. He saw more than the possibly valid motives of those who were complaining. (Perhaps Zacchaeus had swindled them!) Jesus went past all that: without criticism and bitterness seeing only the heart of one who wanted to see, the blindness of an anguished man.

Jesus says to him:

Zacchaeus, hurry and come down, for I must stay at your house TODAY (Luke 19:5).

This "stay at your house" is the same verb, "stay," "remain" which Luke places on the lips of the pilgrims on the Emmaus road after the Resurrection: "they pressed him to stay with them" (Luke 24:29). That which they ask for is offered beforehand to Zacchaeus.

Zacchaeus rejoiced even to meet Jesus (verse 6); at the end of the encounter how happy he must have been when—met with his change of conduct, giving half of his goods to the poor, paying back four times the amount he had stolen—Jesus said: "TODAY salvation has come to this house, because this man too is a son of Abraham." And the text continues "for the Son of Man came to seek out and save the lost." (verse, 10 cf Ezekiel 34:16). Jesus reveals himself as the Good Shepherd (cf. John 10).

Zacchaeus, a rich man engaged in a real, vital and unfettered search, has done what was impossible for the rich man whose search was more one of intellectual curiosity, with conditions placed on how he would receive what Jesus told him. (cf. Luke 18:23). Jesus responds to his humility. **TODAY** salvation has come says Jesus, because this person who appears to others in his society as rich actually is poor, is blind, and in need of the **TODAY** of salvation as a son of Abraham. The Son of Man came to seek out and save what was lost. "What is impossible for humans is possible for God. (Lk 18:27)."

Translated from Spanish by Susan Ferguson. This article appeared in the Fall 1999 edition of **Forum Focus.**

Maria Teresa Porcile Santiso was the Canadian Churches' Forum international visitor in February 1999. She is from Montevideo, Uruguay where she teaches at the Roman Catholic Diocesan Seminary.

4

Practising Jubilee: Leviticus 25:1-17 and Luke 4:16-30

Rev. Edwin Searcy

I first preached a sermon almost thirty years ago from this same pulpit. So it is indeed a special privilege to be 'back home' at West Burnaby United Church and here in Westminster Presbytery. It was all those years ago that you confirmed my call by naming me a Candidate for Ministry. Can it be that I am already well past the age that my father was when he completed his ministry here at West Burnaby twenty-nine years ago to this very day? Now I find myself invited to speak a word at this special celebration of the Jubilee—and not just any word but the Word—the Word of God. Even after all these years—perhaps because of all of these years—I feel more anxious and nervous about such speech than ever. It's not just the 'nerves' that come when preaching to respected friends and colleagues. It is, even more, the sheer terror that always comes when I imagine the enormity of the task. The Word of God, from my lips. It would be funny, if it wasn't a joke. When I wondered aloud with a colleague why I had been so foolish as to say yes to the request from the Presbytery he laughed. Then he said that when the baseball manager walks from the dugout to the pitching mound, takes the ball from the starting pitcher and points to you, warming up in the bullpen, you say 'Give me the ball'. Even if you walked five straight batters last time out!" Let's pray to God for a strike!

To be honest with you, I have been wondering about these texts ever since Vas Saklikar invited me to preach at this event all those months ago. "The theme will be Jubilee," he said. Jubilee. It seemed appropriate. Everyday in the church mail there seems to be more information about Jubilee. In the *United Church Observer*, in our Mission magazine *Mandate*, in reports from the World Council of Churches 8th Assembly last winter. And more. Even the mainstream media—news outlets like the *National Post* and the *Globe and Mail*—have reported the church's year of Jubilee and the campaign for debt relief. You must have heard about this by now, about the global campaign to convince the world's richest nations and banks to free the world's poorest nations from the crushing burdens of debt that continue to grind our brothers and sisters into the ground while our economies reap the benefits. It fits so well with the slogan I learned so long ago in this church. "Live love" we said then. "Live love." It seemed to catch the mood of the late '60s and the mood of Jesus from Nazareth for that matter. The problem with 'living love' is that it's easier said than done, or so we who were teens in the 60s' learned as we grew up. That's where these ancient texts come in. They outline a process for living love. It is right here in Leviticus, once every fifty years is to be called a Jubilee, a year of setting everything straight, giving back property, forgiving debt, placing everyone on an equal footing. Well, some would say, that's in the Old Testament. It is one of those laws that has been done away with in the New Testament. Except that Jesus—wouldn't you know it—stands up in his home congregation and "proclaims the year of the Lord's favour." What, you ask, is the year of the Lord's favour? That's right: the year of Jubilee. The year that is good news to the poor and release to the captives and sight for the blind and freedom for the oppressed. There they are. In red letters in the Bible.

Jesus said it, this I know, for the Bible tells me so.

So, you see, I have been wondering about these texts. Wondering because I can't see any way to wiggle out of them for you. No matter how I try to avoid it I cannot help but hear them say that God is calling God's people to practice Jubilee. It's there in the law. It's there in the prophets. And it is unmistakably there in Jesus the Christ. So why isn't it there in the church? That is what I have been asking myself ever since I said 'yes' to preaching this evening. Why isn't Jubilee practised in the church? Oh, the church is calling on the nations to practice Jubilee. And that's a good thing because if it is good for God's people Israel and good for the church of Jesus Christ then surely it is good for God's world. But, still, what is stopping us, you and me, from practising Jubilee? It seems straightforward enough. Take a sabbatical from work. Live off of the fat of the land for a year. Return all property. Cancel all debts. In other words, give acquisition and consumption a rest. As near as is possible, return things to their original state. See the wisdom in this: God is not ignorant. Humans are very quickly mired in debt while others are captive to their wealth. Every fifty years it is about time to level the playing field and start again. Anyone who has found themselves at the losing end of an endless game of Monopoly knows the gift of starting afresh on even terms!

The hard truth is that we cannot 'do' Jubilee because we are people who don't really know what Jubilee is. We've never done it. We've never practised it. We haven't warmed up. And now we find ourselves in the on-deck circle as the God of Jubilee calls 'batter up!'. It is not in our nature to voluntarily practice Jubilee, to let go of privilege and give away wealth that is inevitably accumulated at other's expense. Just witness the church's great anxiety in the face of the legal, financial and moral fallout from our involvement in the In-dian Residential School system. So I tried another tack. I decided to figure out, as best as I could, why Jubilee this year? I mean, maybe we can put this whole thing off for a year or two. Maybe when Jesus an-nounces the acceptable year of the Lord he doesn't mean 'this' year. If I'm not mistaken there's a 98% chance that this isn't the year of Jubilee. Sure enough, there is nothing in Leviticus or in Luke that points to 1998, the year of Jubilee announced by the World Council of Churches (in marking its fiftieth year) nor to the year 2000 the year of Jubilee announced by the Pope for celebration by the world's Catholics. Instead, Leviticus lays out a carefully prescribed regimen for determining when to celebrate the year of Jubilee. It says to begin counting down the fifty years with a Sabbath day.

That's right. Begin, says the Word of God, with a Sabbath day. Begin not by calling on others to legislate Jubilee. Begin by being a Jubilee people who live a Jubilee life, right here, this Sunday night. Begin by doing 24 hours of nothing that begins with 'ought,' 'should' or 'must'. Once a week. Begin by stopping doing. Begin with rest. That's an order. Can you imagine? Can you imagine us, taking twenty-four hours to do nothing that we have to do. No laundry. No cooking. No housework of any kind by anyone in the house. No bills.

No paying taxes. No homework. None. And no church work either. No meetings. No planning. No organising. It is God's will. Imagine. Twenty-four hours for God. Twenty-four hours to enjoy God. That's what my local Rabbi tells me. Sabbath is time to sleep, to eat good food and drink good wine, to worship, to play, to walk, to be. Time for discussion about things that matter, and time for silence and prayer. Imagine. It sounds so wonderful, so tantalising, so necessary. And yet, have you noticed, inner voices have already begun to say: "It can't be done, it's not possible, it's unrealistic, it's too hard." No wonder the church does not practice Jubilee. We can hardly imagine practising even one Sabbath day never mind a Sabbath year of Jubilee. Do you see? If we cannot obey God by practising Jubilee on such a small scale once a week we will surely never be in shape for the ultimate season of obedience to the God of Jubilee.

There is good reason that the year of Jubilee is fifty years in the making. It takes that much practice. Jubilee takes way more practice time than it took Wayne Gretzky to make the NHL, so much more practice than it took Karen Kain to become a prima ballerina. Fifty years of weekly practice, one Sabbath at a time. Practising over and over again that nothing, not even our precious time nor cherished property belongs to us. Week after week of practising letting go of control over 'getting ahead'. Then notice that every seventh year is to be a 'mini-jubilee'. Every seventh year is to be a sabbatical year. A year to let the crops lie fallow, to let the church meetings rest, to give the earth and our lives time to restore. Let's see, seven times seven years, equals two thousand five hundred and forty-eight Sabbath practices along with seven sabbatical years before being ready to proclaim the 'acceptable year of the Lord.' Hey, we're off the hook. We don't have to worry about Jubilee until, let's see, May 30th, 2048. I'll meet you back here, alright?

I imagine that about now some of you, especially those who are part of the planning team for this event, must be feeling that you made a terrible mistake in inviting me here tonight. After all, it sounds like: (a) I've just written off the debt cancellation campaign for the next fifty years and (b) that I have actually been foolish enough to call the church to submit its life to recovering Sabbath practice for the next half-century! Well, to be clear, it seems to me that any of us who seek to subject our lives to the discipline of biblical faith cannot be anything but the strongest of supporters of any proposal to obey God's Jubilee intentions for the earth, especially the initiative to free the oppressed from the crushing burden of debt. And sending the letters to Canada's Minister of Finance which are available here this evening seems the very least of what we can and must do in support of this dream. But, having said that, we cannot be surprised if the world—which does not subscribe to the laws of the Torah or claim Jesus as its Lord—will consider such initiatives folly. In truth, such a world will only learn the wisdom of the ways of God when it witnesses a people who actually live these ways. Which, if you haven't guessed already, means that practice for Jubilee begins here and now, with this Sabbath worship, with these songs and prayers, with this time and with our resources freely given to God's work in the world. It will continue as we rediscover, week by disciplined week, and year by disciplined year, to live our lives in obedience to the One who proclaims the day and the year of the Lord's favour.

A teacher of mine, Walter Brueggemann, likes to say that God's Word does not come to us in sermons that sound like memos. He says that God's Word is poetic language that moves like a good fast ball, that jumps in front of the batter at just the right moment, breaking open old ways of seeing the world, surprising the church with its abrasion and pace.[1]

"Strike one."

West Burnaby United Church, Burnaby, British Columbia, May 30, 1999. Westminster Presbytery Annual Service of Praise.

Edwin Searcy is minister at University Hill Congregation of the United Church of Canada on the campus of the University of British Columbia in Vancouver, B.C . He is currently a student in the Gospel and Culture specialisation of the Doctor of Ministry program at Columbia Theological Seminary in Decatur, Georgia.

---

[1] Walter Brueggemann, *Finally Comes the Poet*, Minneapolis: Fortress Press:, 1989, 3.

5

The Unforgiving Servant or the Forgiving King: Matthew 18.21-35[1]

Sylvia C. Keesmaat

How often should I forgive my brother if he sins against me?" asks Peter, "As many as seven times?" "Not seven times" answers Jesus, "but seventy-seven (or seventy times seven) times." Even the more conservative seventy-seven is quite an enormous number. But, of course, the exact number is not the issue here. The number seven is the number of fulfilment and, more importantly, the number of Sabbath. Every seven years debt is to be forgiven (Deut 15), every seven times seven is the year of jubilee, when slaves are to be freed as well (Lev 25). Freeing from slavery in the ancient world is in fact a matter of debt forgiveness, since one became a slave if one was unable to pay one's debts. The emphasis on seventy times seven here, then, would evoke the sabbatical forgiveness of Israel's past.

In addition, in the first century the language of forgiveness of sins is language that speaks to the deepest hopes of the people, for it is language that signals return from exile (Wright, *Jesus and the Victory of God,* 268). When Jesus repeatedly forgave the sins of those who came to him for healing, he not only undermined the authority of the temple priests (who were the only ones authorized to perform the sacrifices which resulted in forgiveness), he also evoked the great promises of the dawn of God's new age as they were found in Israel's scriptures. All three of the great visionary prophets, Isaiah, Jeremiah and Ezekiel, describe God's restoration of the people in terms of return to the land, where they will experience safety, fruitfulness and forgiveness. The language used is that of the new exodus, for it is in the exodus that God decides that his way of dealing with this wayward people will be through forgiveness (see Exod 32-34).

So, for example, Jeremiah's description of the new covenant in chapter 31 ends with the affirmation that "they shall all know me, from the least of them to the greatest, says the Lord; for I will forgive their

---

[1] This paper is excerpted from "Strange Neighbours and Risky Care," in *The Challenge of Jesus' Parables*, ed. Richard Longenecker, (Grand Rapids: Eerdmans, forthcoming).

iniquity and remember their sin no more" (Jer 31.34). Similarly, in Jeremiah's vision of restoration, God proclaims:

> I will bring [to Jerusalem] recovery and healing; I will heal them and reveal to them abundance of prosperity and security. I will restore the fortunes of Judah and fortunes of Israel, and rebuild them as they were at first. I will cleanse them from all their guilt of sin against me, and I will forgive all the guilt of their sin and rebellion against me. And this city shall be to me a name of joy, a praise and glory before all the nations of the earth who shall hear of all the good that I do for them; they shall fear and tremble because of all the good and all the prosperity I provide for it (Jer 33.6-11).

And while Ezekiel records the magnificent vision of sprinkling clean water on the people and giving them a heart of flesh for their heart of stone (Ezek 36.25), Isaiah prophecies a servant who will make many righteous by bearing their iniquities (Isa 53.11-12).

All of these passages were central to first century expectations; they are echoed not only throughout the gospels but throughout Paul's letters as well (Keesmaat, *Paul and His Story*). Moreover, the actions of the rebels who took over the temple during the Jewish revolt indicate that expectations of God's new kingdom would include forgiveness of debt. One of the first things the rebels did was to burn the records of debt in the temple treasury (Josephus, *Jewish War* 2.426-27). When Jesus, therefore, began not only to forgive sins but also to proclaim such forgiveness as a defining characteristic of the kingdom and those within it, his hearers would have heard the fulfilment of God's great promises as they are found in both the Torah and the prophetic literature.

In such a context, therefore, it is no surprise that Jesus launches into a parable about debt in response to a question concerning forgiveness. "The kingdom of heaven may be compared to a king who wished to settle accounts with his servants." Notice that the context assumes that the king will be dealing with all of his servants here. He begins this process of accounting with a servant who owed ten thousand talents. Considering the fact that Herod's annual income was nine hundred talents and that all the taxes collected in Galilee and Perea together amounted to two hundred talents annually, ten thousand talents is equivalent to millions of dollars of debt (Ringe, 203). The number is so astronomical that it was impossible to repay, and as the servant could not pay, the Lord ordered him sold. That is, this man along with his wife and children was to become a slave; he was to be sold into slavery. When the servant promised the impossible, to try to pay off the debt, the Lord had compassion and released him and forgave the multi-million dollar debt.

While the numbers are astronomical, the situation of impossibly high debt was one that was altogether too common in the first century. As quite a number of studies have shown, the heavy burden of taxation in first century Israel ensured that many farmers lost their land and therefore their income. Not only, however, was debt common, but the impossibility of emerging out of it was increasingly common as well.

For although Israel's torah demanded that debt be forgiven every seven years, some of the Pharisees had set up a legal fiction called *prozbul* which enabled the holder of a debt to give the debt over to the courts. Because it was then no longer a personal debt, it did not have to be forgiven in the seventh year. One of the reasons given for the law was that creditors were not lending in the sixth year, because they knew that the next year they would have to forgive their loan. On the face of it, therefore, finding a way around debt forgiveness supposedly opened up credit. The end result, however, was the perpetuation of debt in the land, since such a law leads to increased incidents of foreclosure rather than forgiveness (for the relevant texts see Neusner I.217-222). Interestingly, this also provides evidence that the 7th year sabbatical for debt was practised in the first century, or else such a legal fiction would be unnecessary.

So Jesus set up a scenario here that was—at first—entirely plausible and believable for first century Jews. They knew all too well how such stories unfold in their context: a lord or landowner decides to finally settle his accounts and foreclose on his debtors. Those who owe him money end up losing their land and they themselves, along with their wives, sons and daughters, all end up becoming slaves.

Incredibly, in Jesus' kingdom these stories turn out differently. The servant begs and pleads for time and what is granted him is release from slavery and total forgiveness of debt. Coming after all those sabbath numbers, the overtones are unmistakable. This is a king who has pro-

claimed jubilee for this servant. After all, the Sabbath and Jubilee legislation (Deut 15 and Lev 25) were for precisely this sort of situation, one
of impossibly high debt that could not be paid off. Jesus' hearers would
have heard, with ever-increasing joy, that this kingdom that Jesus proclaimed was indeed a fulfilment of the Mosaic law. Jubilee was—finally—being enacted.

Now the story could have continued with the king. After all, we
have been told that he wished to settle accounts with all of his servants.
Presumably he continued to deal with the other servants as he had dealt
with the first, proclaiming a gracious release and forgiveness beyond
anyone's wildest expectation or hope. But that is not where the story
goes, for the action shifts to the forgiven servant. Now that he has
experienced this great jubilee event, now that he has discovered that the
world of this kingdom is one of graciousness and forgiveness, how will
he live in that kingdom? Now that he has discovered the true nature of
the lord he serves, will he in turn display that nature to anyone else?
Having discovered the graciousness that is at the heart of this kingdom,
will he live out this "economy of grace" himself? (Ringe 202) Well, you
know the answer. The forgiven servant, coming upon a fellow servant
who owed him a few hundred denarii, which is approximately 10,000
dollars in today's terms, refuses to cut him any slack when he cannot
pay, and throws him into prison.

This forgiven servant has not got the point. He has not figured out
that now he lives in a kingdom that operates by completely different
rules, by a completely different law, and so he acts as though he were
still in the old regime. To put it in the terms of Israel's scriptures, this
servant is acting like he is still in Egypt rather than the promised land.
His failure to forgive shocks his fellow servants—some of whom,
presumably, have also just had their debts forgiven—and as a result they
report him to the king. His punishment is far worse than his original
enslavement would have been. So, says Jesus, your heavenly father will
do to you if you do not forgive your brother and sister from the heart.

What kind of a world does the story of this parable create? One
that is far beyond the expectation of most first century Jews, but maybe
not beyond their wildest hopes. For just as the language of forgiveness
indicated the fulfilment of the restoration of the people and God's
presence with them once again, so the language of debt forgiveness

indicated a new order in which economic liberation was indeed experienced and where the people were slaves no more. Such hope of wide-ranging forgiveness was deeply rooted in Israel's scriptures.

Interpretation of this parable has tended, throughout the centuries, to drive a wedge between forgiveness of sins and forgiveness of debt in actual concrete terms. Indeed, the argument could easily be summarised like this: "the Jewish people of Jesus' day expected a messiah who would come and release them from bondage to the Romans and would forgive all their debts. Jesus, however, proclaimed a more radical message than they could imagine, since he proclaimed forgiveness of *sins* rather than mere monetary debt. In pinning their hope on the forgiveness of monetary debt, the Jews show how mistaken they were in their thinking." The end result of such a dualist reading of the gospel (and of such a misreading of first century Judaism) is that many readers of this text have been able to separate forgiveness of sin and forgiveness of debt as if the former is a christian concern and the latter is not.

But the evidence of the gospel is entirely otherwise. Throughout the scriptures and the story of Jesus' ministry, the two are always intertwined. In Israel's scriptures, forgiveness of sin and redemption from slavery was the hallmark of God's dealing with the covenant people. Moreover, forgiveness of debt was central to how such forgiveness and redemption were to be manifest in the community God called together to bear his image.

So, as I have indicated, the Israelites were to forgive debts and free slaves every seven years (Deut 15). In fact, the law culminates in the jubilee year, where a total economic levelling was to take place involving release of slaves and return of land as well (Lev 25). Slavery and loss of land, of course, were almost always the result of debt in the first place. Such laws were rooted in Israel's memory of her God: because God releases slaves out of Egyptian bondage, so Israel is called to image that God by being a slave releasing community (Deut 15.15). Such texts show that in the new covenant reality to which God calls God's people, forgiveness extends far beyond the personal to the social and economic spheres of life. Not only does God's covenantal reign proclaim a radically new way of being in our so-called "spiritual" lives, but God's reign also proclaims a new beginning socially and economically. One cannot proclaim the reign of God and not practice that reign in every area of life.

When Nehemiah returns to the land with the Israelites who had been exiled it becomes clear that this issue of indebtedness is one that is threatening the very fabric of their community. So Nehemiah proclaims that all interest taking is to stop and all debt forgiven, that is, all fields, vineyard and olive orchards are to be restored (Neh 5.1-13). Shortly thereafter, when the people pledge themselves once again to the covenant, there are four main things they pledge themselves to: no intermarriage, no buying on the Sabbath, the giving of tithes, and the forgoing of crops and the forgiveness of debt every seventh year (Neh 10: 28-39). Clearly the issue of debt and forgiveness was seen as a defining characteristic of what it was to be the people of God.

Those who came into contact with Jesus seem to have interpreted his message in just this way. Zaccheus, upon receiving Jesus into his home, promises to give half of his possessions to the poor and return fourfold anything he took through cheating (Luke 19.1-10). The rich young man is told to sell all that he has, give the money to the poor and follow Jesus in order to inherit eternal life (Mark 10.17-31). And both Matthew and Luke in their tellings of the Lord's prayer explicitly link forgiveness of monetary debt and forgiveness of sin. Matthew does this by recording the prayer: "forgive us our debts, as we forgive our debtors" (*opheiletas*) and comments on this petition in terms of forgiveness of sin (*paraptomata*). Luke, even more strikingly, records "forgive us our sins (*hamartias*), for we forgive all who are indebted (*opheilonti*) to us." The Greek word used for debt in both of these texts is one that means economic debt. The forgiveness of sin is, therefore, linked explicitly to the forgiving of economic debt.

The early church, too, seems to have interpreted Jesus in this way. We see in Acts 2.44-47 that Pentecost resulted in the newly baptised community selling all that they had to share with those in need. There is here an economic levelling fully consistent with the intent of Jubilee. And Paul's call to an economic sharing amongst the churches is rooted in the same ethos (see especially 2 Cor 8,9; cf. James 1.27; 2.15).

Clearly then, Jesus has told a story which has drawn deeply from the scriptures of Israel, and which has indicated that the central aspects of the new age have dawned: forgiveness of sin and forgiveness of debt.

Moreover, in telling this story he has drawn his listeners into this world, and described a reality that they must either accept or reject.

Jesus is preaching a message which presents a threat to the wealthy and the landowners, who have no desire to forgive the debts of their slaves, and a message of profound joy and liberation for slaves, debtors, the poor.

Which brings us, of course, to the question of our place in such a world. Where do we fit in this story; how does it become ours? One thing is clear: our very presence in this room places us firmly on the list of those who should be most threatened by this parable. This is hard for us to comprehend sometimes—the contexts are so different. We live in a much larger world, a global world, where the debts people suffer from most are national not personal, where lack of forgiveness results in nuclear detonations in Asia.

In such a context, what does Jesus' radical message proclaim? How do these parables invite us to repentance and to live in this radical kingdom? Who are we? Are we the people who in spite of the forgiveness of our debts, both "spiritual" and "economic" insist on payment from others; whether that be holding a grudge in our homes or churches or holding the debts of the South over their heads? Or do we practice God's gracious forgiveness in our churches, homes and world, joining in with initiatives like Jubilee 2000, which is seeking to forgive the debt of the poorest nations? Are we proclaiming this new world of radical forgiveness or denying it?

In a world of crippling international debt that is paid literally with the lives and health of the poorest of the poor and the sacrifice of the world's eco-systems, this parable proclaims a radically alternative world characterised by Jubilee. In a world in which the very truth of the gospel is continually undermined by scandalous schism and enmity in the church, Jesus tells stories that can only be heard and understood when the listening community is suffused with a compassion that is manifest in gracious forgiveness on all levels of our societal and personal lives.

Sylvia Keesmaat is Assistant Professor of Biblical Studies and Hermeneutics at the Institute for Christian Studies.

Selected Bibliography

Capon, Robert Farrar
   1988   *The Parables of Grace*. Grand Rapids: Eerdmans, 1988.
   Josephus ed. H. St.J. Thackeray, R. Marcus A. Wikgren and L.H.
   Feldman. Loeb Classical Library, 9 vols (London: Heinemann;
   Cambridge, Mass: Harvard University Press, 1926-1965).

Keesmaat, Sylvia C.
   (forthcoming)   *Paul and His Story: (Re)Interpreting the Exodus
   Tradition*. Sheffield: Sheffield Academic Press.

Neusner, Jacob
   1971   *The Rabbinic Traditions About the Pharisees Before 70*. 3
   Volumes. Leiden: Brill.

Ringe, Sharon H.
   1995   "Solidarity and Contextuality: Readings of Matthew
   18.21-35" in *Reading from this Place. Vol 1: Social Location and
   Biblical Interpretation in the United States*. Eds: Fernando F. Se-
   govia and Mary Ann Tolbert. Minneapolis: Fortress Press,
   199-212.

Wilder, Amos N.
   1991   "Story and Story-World" in *The Bible and the Literary
   Critic*. Minneapolis: Fortress, 132-148.

Wright, N Thomas
   1997   *Jesus and the Victory of God*. Minneapolis: Fortress Press.

6

Reflections on the Economic Model in the Light of Luke 19:11-27

Alejandro Zorzin

The one who has will always be given more, but the one who has not will forfeit even what he has. (Lk 19.26)

We live in times in which the economic model known by some as neo-liberalism and by others as market globalisation seems to have become the only standard of truth for socio-political decision-making by our governments. The economic efficiency of the system of production, finance and taxes, as measured by the greatest possible reduction in spending (including cuts to the wages of those still employed), combined with the greatest possible increase in profits (for investors) is the only standard used to decide how much adjustment to apply, and where to invest or not to invest.

But like all truths which claim to be absolute, it brooks no discussion. Anyone who tries to discuss economic and political matters is forced to accept this premise that economic logic is the only valid basis for discussion. Anyone who refuses to accept the premise or who does not accept that supply and demand imposed by the unstable world capital market is the only sensible argument seems to have no right to express an opinion or to be heard.

However, and at the risk of being labelled "crazy," we must dare to discuss the validity of this pre-condition being imposed on us, especially because the effects of this logic are devastating. One example of this is that in the middle of "stability," the world market is pushing up the price of grains. Accordingly on the Argentine pampa (breadbasket to the world), the market price of flour doubles, and the price of our daily bread also climbs to twice the price.

We must wonder, as Protestants, are we just going along with those who spout this reasoning? Spiritually, must we also go along with savage adjustment programs? Does the Bible have nothing to say about this? Is it possible that Jesus Himself was unaffected by such problems or that they did not exist in His time?

Economic Efficiency and its Consequences

At first glance, Jesus seems to have been realistic enough to recognize the economic laws which regulated society and politics in the Palestine of His day. Why else would He have said that those who had would always be given more, while those who have not will forfeit even what they have? (See Matthew 13:12 and 25:29.) Is it not true that since the world began, poor people become ever poorer and the rich richer? His observations about the owners of the vineyards able to take advantage of the "army of unemployed" who wait in the square all day to be paid their single dinar (Matthew 20:1-15) seem also to validate the current economic model; likewise the example of the rich farmers of Galilee, whose silos were filled to bursting with crops (Luke 12:13-21). What other consolation did the poor people of Palestine have, beyond the promise of the future Kingdom of God?

Therefore, if the Lord Himself seems not to have challenged it, why should we also not submit to the immovable law of economic efficiency as a socio-political criterion?

But wait a moment. In the Gospel of Luke we read that when Jesus approached Jerusalem, the people had built up a great expectation that the Kingdom of God was at hand. It appears that many people thought that Jesus, the Messiah King, would assume the political and religious leadership of the capital of Palestine. Given these expectations, Jesus, as usual, told a parable (Luke 19:11-27). A careful re-reading of this parable shows us what Jesus thought of the model of political and economic administration of the day. Furthermore, Luke leaves no doubt about Jesus' harsh criticism of it.

Jesus' parable starts by showing us a person of noble birth, who in order to be crowned the king of the realm, must travel to the capital of the empire (v. 12). He was apparently not loved by his fellow citizens, who immediately sent a delegation to keep him from being named as their king (v. 14). In addition to his political ambitions, this man was the possessor of a considerable fortune. He charged ten employees with the care of his business during his absence (v.13).

His travel in search of political power was successful and he returned with the royal title. He immediately called his employees to review each ones handling of the business matters entrusted to him. As a new king, he needed a team of administrators to look after his land, and he used his employees' demonstrated economic efficiency as the criterion for assigning the new duties. The sharpest of them had turned a profit of one thousand percent. No one asks how he managed this "economic miracle"—the numbers speak for themselves. The man was undoubtedly an excellent administrator, capable of looking after the collections and revenues generated by ten cities: he would be able to get one hundred cities' performance out of them (v. 15-17)! But they were not all so efficient. We are told that a second servant was "only" able to produce a return of 500 percent. But he too would be a useful addition to the team of governors, whose task was to invest, risk and earn exorbitant sums. Economic efficiency determined political reasoning.

But the line of successful executives came to a sudden end. The story presents us next with a fearful loser, a servant who had earned nothing, who was not efficient. Why? Apparently because he understood his master's way of thinking. The new king was the sort who drew out what he had never put in and reaped what he had not sown (v.20-21). His ethics were not based on work and production, but rather on financial speculation on parallel circuits. He was accustomed to profiting from what actually belonged to others.

Confronted with this fact, the new king furiously upbraided the employee for his ineptitude. He was so useless that he didn't even know how to take a reasonable risk and invest the capital in the official financial circles. If he had deposited the money in a bank he would have at least received some return (beginning at v.22). Someone like this was of no use to the economic model the political plans of the new monarch relied on. Thus, the king fired him, but not before taking back the little the man had, to give it to the one who had more. An obvious move, because the other man would be able to build up the capital efficiently—by investing outside the normal financial institutions.

The king's attitude was so harsh that his erstwhile colleagues felt a touch of solidarity with the poor loser. "My lord, are you not going a bit too far, giving more to one who already has much, and not allowing this man who had hardly anything a second try (v.24)?" But they could not reach the king, for the logic of economic efficiency is immune to this line of reasoning. Capital has no heart or homeland. There is no room in this model for sentimentality. And, in case there was any doubt about the basis of his economic and political plans, the new king explained his reasoning: "the one who has will always be given more; but the one who has not will forfeit even what he has. (beginning at v. 26)." Those who are able to multiply their start-up capital (and the method is of no importance, be it from money that was never invested or from a harvest one risked nothing to produce) will be rewarded by the system by gaining greater political office. Those who generate no exorbitant profits will suffer the consequences.

At this point in the story, one must wonder, "what consequences can one expect from such a model whose only yardstick is the unbridled profits yielded by an investment system with short and medium term returns of a thousand or five hundred percent?" Jesus leaves no doubt about the answer. In the final passage of this terrible parable, we find the answer: the final consequences of this approach is extreme political violence, state terrorism. Citizens who opposed the model (only at this point do we learn why people did not want this man for their king) are ordered to be put to death (v.27). The ultimate consequence of economic logic-cum-socio-political rules is violence exercised by the seat of power against those who dare to dissent: "bring them here and slaughter them in my presence."

An Anti-Gospel Model

The Word of God, Jesus' parable, as conveyed to us by Luke, takes us by surprise. Looking at it from this perspective sends chills up our spines. It is not hard to see why Jesus was executed. Someone who stands at the doors of big capital and so openly dares to unmask the inhumane logic of the political reasoning the rulers applied with the backing of the Temple—turned into a robbers' cave (see Luke 19:45-

48)—ends up being a dangerous enemy of the system. Jesus was able to overturn the values and logic that underpinned the model of Pax Romana. From the depths of His faith, He radically challenged the idea that those who have not must forfeit what little they have to live on and turn it over to those who have much, who profit further by speculation. For the Jesus Luke knew, this economic and political model based on injustice could only engender violence: it was anti-Kingdom.

Therefore, if the Gospel only confirmed our view of reality, if the Word of God revealed by Jesus Christ only helped us confirm the cruel and anguishing world we live in, it would not be Good News. God challenges and criticises the order of things we hold as irreversible. God is far from acceptance of an approach which has such destructive effects on society. Furthermore, the words of Jesus question this approach to the core.

God does not support money speculation or the 'culture of waste' (a consequence of the former) as a Protestant lifestyle. God does not identify with investors who reap where they have not sown, and shamelessly demand payment on loans they never made. The Gospel continues to be good news, especially because it does not support the savage logic of economic efficiency. We should thus reject the premise advanced as a pre-condition to the debate.

The peace of God is incompatible with a more or less subtle form of economic violence which turns those who have little into those who have less and less while those who have more than they need get more than ever. Because God is God and His Kingdom does not conform to this model, as Christians and Protestants we must protest, speaking out about our disagreement with the model of economic efficiency as the only criterion for the design of the future of our countries and our children.

Translation from Spanish by Daina Green.

Dr. Alejandro Zorzin, is a pastor in Buenos Aires, Argentina at the Iglesia Evangélica del Río de la Plata. He also teaches Church History at the Instituto Superior Evangélico De Estudios Teológicos.

7

An Outcast's Vision

Joanne Clarke.

The story of Hagar and Ishmael, so effectively told this morning thanks to David Craig's wonderful use of drama, is a disturbing tale. Sarah and Abraham, members of God's chosen people, cast out their slave Hagar and her child Ishmael— Abraham's own son. They send them into the desert with almost nothing where the two will likely die. As I see it, however, this story is also one of vision and hope—a tale so fitting for our time. I invite you, therefore, to join me in journeying through Hagar's story from Genesis one more time now and to explore its message for us today.

Sarah, the wife of Abraham, was aging and was unable to bear a child. Meanwhile, God had promised Abraham that he would become a "Father of a Great Nation." Abraham needed an heir but Sarah was unable to provide one for him. Enter Hagar, Sarah's Egyptian slave-girl. She was of child-bearing age. She was the property of Abraham and Sarah and was forced to become Abraham's concubine—forced to have sex with her master against her wishes. She conceived and, during her pregnancy with Abraham's child, Hagar ran away in fear. Sarah was jealous of Hagar and her wrath was increasingly hard for Hagar to bear. But God spoke to Hagar and told her to go back to Sarah. Indeed, numerous Biblical scholars note that God's discussion with Hagar, as outlined in Genesis, is the first instance in the Bible in which God speaks directly to anyone.

So what did God have to say to this young female slave? "You will give birth to a child of promise," God assured Hagar. "You will name your son Ishmael which means 'God hears'... God hears you, Hagar, and God will hear Ishmael, and from you will come a great nation of many people." This was God's promise to Hagar. And so, Hagar returned to Sarah and gave birth to Ishmael. At last, Abraham had an heir. Sometime after Ishmael's birth, however, Sarah, an elderly woman of 91 by that time, miraculously became pregnant and gave birth to Isaac. As Sarah saw it, Isaac was Abraham's true heir— it was Isaac who should receive Abraham's inheritance. Ishmael's presence increasingly disturbed Sarah. And so, Sarah requested that

Abraham send Hagar and Ishmael into the desert. God told Abraham that Isaac would also become a great nation—that it would be through Isaac that offspring would be named for Abraham. In other words, God's promise for Isaac was almost the same as that which God had earlier promised for Ishmael. And so, Abraham banished Hagar and Ishmael into the desert with nothing more than a bit of bread and a skin of water. Of course, it was not long before the bread and water were gone. In desperation, Hagar put Ishmael in the shade of some bushes and moved some distance away from her dying child. Sitting there, her child close to death, Hagar must have felt totally betrayed by God who had promised so much for Ishmael and for her. "Do not let me look on the death of the child," cried Hagar, as she called out to God through her tears. And suddenly, God spoke out to Hagar saying, "What's the problem, Hagar? Do not be afraid. I hear the cries of your child. Lift him up Hagar and hold him." Upon opening her eyes, Hagar saw a well of water—fresh, life-giving water. Quickly, she filled the water skin and quenched the thirst of her dying child. And, in the end, Ishmael thrived and went on to lead a great Arab nation. And God's promise was fulfilled for both Ishmael and Isaac—and for their parents.

It is very easy to hear this story and simply comment on the apparent viciousness of Sarah and weakness of Abraham, and to dismiss their actions as cruel and ungrateful. However, to understand the motives behind Sarah's behaviour, as well as Abraham's, we must analyze their actions within the context of their time. Let's take a look, therefore, at the social dynamics at work within Ancient Mediterranean Society—within the Hebrew world of Abraham and Sarah.

One of the main forces at work within Ancient Greek, Roman and Judaic cultures was the social value of honour and shame. To put it simply, men had honour and women had shame. A man's honour was tied up with his birth, his family of origin, with his name and with his gender. This is how a man defined his social self. A woman had no honour except through the family into which she married and through her ability to bear children. Abraham's honour, therefore, was tied heavily to the fulfillment of God's promise of becoming a "Father of a Great nation." Without an heir, all honour would be gone for Abraham—without an heir, this great family of honour, this respected lineage, the family name, and even Abraham's gender would have no meaning. To be the wife of Abraham, the wife of a man from such a respected family would surely have brought honour to Sarah. But their entire world would have been watching and waiting for an heir. To be without child would have brought the very worst shame on Sarah and upon the entire family. Sarah would have been perceived as a failure.

It was natural that Abraham and Sarah were slave-owners because they lived in an imperialistic, slave-based economy. To force Hagar to become Abraham's concubine would not have been unusual for social relations of that time. This is not to deny the abusiveness of such treatment. However, we must read this story within the socio-economic context of that time and the sense of the Ancient Mediterranean social values of honour and shame. There were social forces at work that shaped this story, and the actions of Sarah and Abraham. These same social forces created Hagar and Ishmael's reality.

Where, then, are the Hagars and Ishmaels of today's world? Where are the Sarahs and Abrahams and Isaacs? And what are the socio-economic forces which shape this story as is lived out today?

The Jubilee Call

Indeed, as we worship this morning, the leaders of the richest industrialized nations known as the G-7 (now the G-8) nations are gathering in Cologne, Germany and are expected to announce their decision to provide conditional—and I stress conditional—debt relief to the 36 poorest nations in the world. Canada's Prime Minister is participating in this summit. This conditional debt relief is considered insufficient because it demands that these impoverished nations make further cutbacks to social spending in order to qualify for debt relief. This provision of debt relief, as insufficient as it is, is at least a step in the right direction. And it did not come about out of the goodness of the hearts of the G7 leaders. That would have been like Sarah and Abraham running out into the desert saying, "Oh, we've changed our mind, Hagar, come back and drink from our water and share our bread." Given the social forces at work during Hagar's time, that wasn't going to happen. Given the economic forces at work in today's world, debt relief and economic justice will not come about without increasing pressure from millions of people around the globe. And, indeed, an international movement of people called Jubilee 2000, is calling for long-term transformation involving people of the debtor countries as agents of their own liberation.

During this G7 Cologne Summit which ends today, 10 million signatures from around the world are being presented to the leaders of 8 of the richest nations. These petitions call for debt forgiveness for 52 of the world's poorest nations. Gail Allan, from Trinity St. Paul's, is in Cologne as part of this initiative and is presenting the Canadian signatures totaling more than 635,000. The Hagars of this world, and those who stand with them, are crying out, "We will not sit and watch these children die." Indeed, the deaths of children in these indebted countries have increased tenfold since the International Monetary Fund and the World Bank—the international lending institutions—enforced what's known as Structural Adjustment Programmes (SAPs). SAPs are conditions that poor countries have had to meet in order to pay off their debt—often unjust debts which have accumulated as a result of decades and even centuries of Western exploitation. Just as Hagar's labour was stolen from her in a slave-economy, so too have the wealthy nations stolen land, resources, and capital from the poorest. Let's look at how IMF SAPs work in Mozambique, Africa, for example, or in Haiti, in the Caribbean. These countries are so poor that many families cannot afford to send their children to school. Public education is almost non-existent. Children frequently die from preventable illnesses due to poor health care conditions. With some of the highest rates of child mortality, the rich, who control the IMF and the World Bank, continue to demand that these and other countries pay down their debt by making further cuts to social spending. Cuts to education and health care, for example. Financiers for the IMF and World Bank accept that further deaths of children will have to occur as a necessary consequence of dealing with the debt.

But the Hagars of the world see something much more life-giving. They see a vision of living water. Our church partners in Asia,

Africa, and Latin America and the Caribbean, for example, are continuing to call for debt relief and are insisting that their countries are more involved in decisions around the debt. Millions from other countries around the world are joining in this Jubilee Initiative. Indeed, this week in England, thousands of average British citizens formed a three-mile human chain throughout London with banners which read "Drop the Debt." Similar initiatives are happening all over the world this week and the pressure is expected to increase. People like you and me are rising up and saying "We will not sit and watch these children die." At this point, however, the debt relief offered by the G7 leaders is conditional. When such conditions mean that more children will die, we, as Christians, must say that this is unacceptable. So what are the economic forces at work today which deny the Hagars and Ishmaels the fulfillment of God's promise? Is there not enough money in the rich nations to accommodate total debt relief? According to the May edition of *New Internationalist* magazine, the total debt of the 36 poorest nations, about 50 billion dollars, is far less than the total assets of Bill Gates. The total assets of 300 of the world's billionaires is equal to that of half of the world's population—the lowest half. Five percent of this wealth, if equitably distributed, would alleviate the entire global crisis in housing, education, health care, hunger, and would also enable the provision of clean water for all. Just 5 % of each billionaire's wealth would help to build God's well of living water for all. But the rich refuse to willingly participate in a more equitable distribution of wealth. Indeed, under the heading of global competition, they are actively seeking more cutbacks in taxes and social spending to ensure a further increase in their wealth. And Canada is not removed from this. Our country has the highest per capita rate of billionaires in the world. Hundreds of Ontario-based corporations pay not one penny in income tax. According to the 1996 figures from the Ontario Federation of Labour (OFL), for example, General Motors Canada Ltd, based in Ontario, made close to one billion dollars in profits but paid not one penny in income tax. Meanwhile, more than one and a half million Canadian children live in poverty and that rate continues to rise.

The Hagars of today's world, are moved by a vision of life-giving water. They reject the forces of greed and are working to create a well for all not just for the elite few. We can give thanks for the Hagars in our partner churches around the world and for the Hagars right here at Trinity-St. Paul's. Indeed, if we believe that God's promise is for the Ishmael's of this world—a promise of food, shelter, clean water, health care and education, then what about the Isaac's of today— what about those children whose material needs are met? As we read in Genesis, God's promise was for Isaac too—a boy of privilege. As I see it, many of the children in Canada and in our congregation, are the Isaac's of today's world. While none of the children in Trinity-St. Paul's are rich by the standards of excess wealth discussed here, and indeed, I know there are families amongst us who are struggling to make ends meet, it is, I think, true that our children live in a culture of affluence. They are surrounded by excess, they are told they must have more things to be truly human, They are aggressively sought after as an ever younger group of consumers and competitors.

Voice #2: Jesus said, "Do not think that I have come to bring peace to the earth. I have come not to bring peace, but a sword."

If God's promise is for the Isaacs of this world as well as for the Ishmaels, then how is this promise fulfilled for children who are sur-rounded by excess? I believe that we all suffer spiritually, children included, when we have too much or are even surrounded by too much. When we are not thankful for what we have, we are spiritually impoverished. A Jamaican migrant worker working in the United States expressed this well when he said:

> In Jamaica, we are poor.
> Sometimes I wake up in the morning
> And there is only tea in the house.
> I get down on my knees and say
> "Thank you God for the tea."
> In America, you have so many things
> Yet I am confused.
> I see so much around me, in your country
> But I don't see your people saying
> "Thank you, God."

Again, this is, I believe, the economic forces of our time, shaping the Isaac's of our society. In a consumer-based economy, our children are seen as primary consumers. It does not serve this economy well for our children to be grateful, for them to say, "I have enough." And so, they fall prey to the disease of consumption and are victims of a spiritual crisis of our time. But God's promise is for Isaac as well as Ishmael. It is God's promise that our children also receive fullness of life—not material fullness but spiritual fullness.

Voice #2: And Jesus said, "Those who find their life will lose it, and those who lose their life for my sake will find it. "

Let me close with a story which connects the world of Hagar and Ishmael with the world of Sarah and Isaac. Keyhinge Toy factory in Vietnam, a plant fully owned by a Hong Kong company, produces giveaway toys for Macdonald's fast-food multinational. One thousand workers, mostly young women with children, have been struggling for their rights to minimum wage, working hours, health and safety standards and the right to organize. When these women protest, they are fired. Hundreds of these workers have become seriously ill as a result of chemical poisoning and many have died from these conditions. In a similar toy factory in Southern China, which also produces Macdonald's giveaway toys, the working conditions are so bad that the young women workers are locked inside the factory and steel bars cover the windows. In one such factory, a 1993 fire killed 87 women and injured 47 others. Many children lost their mothers in that fire but, of course, the company provided absolutely no compensation to the families. Here in Canada the signs at the Golden Arches currently boast "99 billion customers served".

After having dinner out last week, my youngest daughter came home with the latest giveaway toy from a Macdonald's Happy Meal—a cell phone in the shape of MacDonald's french fries. This particular toy really bothered me. Perhaps because I am now aware of price people across the world have had to pay to make this useless toy. It's also offensive to me because I am aware now of how it is part of a scheme to manipulate my child. A MacDonald's manager once explained to me how important the toys arc in Macdonald's marketing schemes. They lure the children in along with their parents. When I commented on how useless most of the toys were, this manager said "Well that's the beauty of them. They are fun for a few minutes, they're free so they can throw them away or lose them. Then before you know it, they will want to come back for another one." And so, each toy discarded represents another Hagar and Ishmael cast out into the desert. Every time I buy these happy meals and these toys for my child, I become like Sarah, sending people off into the wilderness without enough to even survive. I can also be like Hagar, strong, nurturing, tenacious Hagar. I can do my bit and tell that Macdonald's manager that I'm concerned about his organization's working conditions. My family can stop eating there until we hear about significant improvements in this restaurant chain. With the 10 million people who signed the petitions for debt relief, I can stand up and say, "I refuse to sit and watch these children die."

Voice #2: And Jesus said, "Those who find their life will lose it, but those who lose their life for my sake will find it. "

I am moved by Hagar's vision. It is a hope-filled vision of life-giving water. Just as Hagar took action by bringing Ishmael to drink at the well, so too can we take action to create a world in which all children have their basic needs met; so too can we take action to create a world in which all children have enough but not too much. Indeed, the obscene wealth of so few alongside the extreme poverty of so many creates a spiritual and an economic crisis for us all. And God's promise was for Isaac as a well as Ishmael, for Hagar as well as Sarah and Abraham. It is a promise of God's Shalom—of wholeness, love, justice, and freedom for all. And so... let us come to the water. Amen.

Preached on June 20th 1999 at Trinity St. Paul's United Church, Toronto.

Joanne Clarke is student at Emmanuel College training for Ministry in the United Church. She is a former animator for the United Church Division of World Outreach.

8

The Homicidal Vineyard Workers

Richard Renshaw, c.s.c.

In Isaiah, 5:1-7 we have the love song for the vineyard. The tender love of God for Israel is rudely returned with "wild grapes" unfit for food. God expected "justice," that is to say that God's Reign of mercy and compassion would be extended throughout the vineyard. But what took place was bloodshed. God expected "righteousness"—an attitude of caring and compassion—and got a " cry of distress" instead.

Isaiah makes it clear in the verse that follows this passage what is the cause of his outrage: "Woe to those who add house to house and join field to field until everywhere belongs to them and they are the sole inhabitants of the land." *(Did you know that the three richest men in the world have enough personal wealth to cancel the debt of the 50 poorest countries? Or that the wealth of the 100 richest Canadians could do the same?)*

Now, in Matthew 21 Jesus quotes the opening words of Isaiah's story word for word. However, the story then takes a turn. It is not the produce of the field that he focuses on but the attitude of those who are in charge of the vineyard. It is not just the bloodshed and distress that is the problem, but the incapacity of the leaders to even hear a call to change. They turn against those who call them to justice: first the prophets and then the Messiah himself. *(Already in our century Mahatma Ghandi, Martin Luther King, Oscar Romero, Bp. Juan Gerardi and thousands more have been murdered. In recent Church teaching, it is the face of the poor and excluded that reveals the face of Christ and the call to conversion).*

In Jesus' story, the vineyard is given to other leaders, a reference to the call of the Gentiles in the early Church. But, in the current context, the danger is much more severe and much closer to that of Isaiah: the entire vineyard may be destroyed! Ours is a tiny, fragile planet.

I don't think there is any need to draw out the implications of a contemporary reading of these texts. Still, I can't let pass the words of James Wolfensohn, President of the World Bank at the annual meeting of the International Monetary Fund in Washington on September 28, 1999:

Per capita incomes ... will stagnate or decline this year in all regions except East and South Asia. In the developing world, with the exception of China, 100 million more people [live] in poverty today than a decade ago. ... 1.5 billion people still [lack] access to safe water and 2.4 million children ... die each year of waterborne diseases. 125 million children [are] still not in primary school. 1.8 million people ... die annually of indoor air pollution... And the forests are being destroyed at the rate of an acre a second... Of the 6 billion [people] today, 3 billion live [on] under $2 a day and 1.3 billion live [on] under $1 a day. ... The number of conflicts seems likely to be higher, the quality of our environment will be worse, the disparities between rich and poor will be wider.

He then went on to say,

We have learned that the causes of financial crises and poverty are one and the same. Countries may come up with sound fiscal and monetary policy, but if they do not have good governance, if they do not confront the issue of corruption, if they do not have a complete legal system which protects human rights, property rights and contracts, which gives a framework for bankruptcy laws and a predictable tax system, if they do not have an open and regulated financial system and appropriate regulation and behaviour that is transparent, their development is fundamentally flawed and will not last.

We live in an extraordinary country at an extraordinary time in world history. Leadership depends on our financial and political leaders. It also depends on the moral voice of our Churches and citizenry that call public leaders to account. The choice is ours. Every time we recite the Lord's Prayer or celebrate the Lord's Supper, we commit ourselves to take a stand. As John Paul II has repeatedly said, "the word for love in the 20th century is solidarity."

Richard Renshaw is Assistant General Secretary of the Canadian Religious Conference.

9

A Jubilee Call for African Women

Omega Bula

A story is told of a pastor in local church in Zambia, who at the end of each three-hour service, stood at the door to greet members of his congregation. One by one they would file past him, shaking hands, and he would ask how they, their children and grandchildren were doing. Many of them, afraid of wasting the pastor's time, would smile, nod their heads and go on their way.

One Sunday, Mama Chanda came up to the Pastor and said:

> You really want to know how I am? How can you ask the question when you see that I live in poverty. Look at me. I have no food. My children are sick and I can't afford to take them to the hospital. We cannot afford medicines. We have buried two of my grandchildren in the last six months. Yesterday, I lost my stand at the market because I can't pay the rent. My income was the only one left after my husband was laid off. Now we have nothing. Many people in this congregation are just like me. Why do you ask us, when you can see with your own eyes the cross we carry? Pastor, it is immoral to make us carry this cross.

She walked away, with tears in her eyes. Those in hearing distance from her nodded their heads, shook the pastor's hand in silence and walked away.

The pastor was shocked to hear so boldly from this woman as she articulated what this dilemma has been for many years: How to enable his congregation to talk about the vicious cycle of poverty, its root causes, its impact on the lives of people, and what individually and together, they can do to break the cycle?[1]

At its independence in 1994, Zambia had the third highest per capita income in Africa. Today, there is one doctor per 7,150, 42% of the population is not expected to survive the age of 40 and 86% of

---

[1] The story of Mama Chanda is written by Omega Bula and was first published in *The Economic Way of the Cross*, the Religious Working Group on the IMF and the World Bank, Washington, D.C., 1996.

the population lives on less than $1 per day. 70% of Zambians work in the informal sector with no regular income. Why? In a country with mineral wealth and other resources like water, forests etc.?[2]

At the root of this cycle of poverty is an economic system that is immoral. It has imprisoned the lives of Mama Chanda and her community, denying them the human rights given equally to all by God. There is a limit to what a struggling African woman like Mama Chanda can do to set herself free from poverty. Much lies beyond her power. It is in the hands of the economic and bureaucratic elite in Zambia and corporate capitals of the world.

This address is a cry and a call from the hearts of African women like Mama Chanda; from the womb of creation groaning in pain; from God's own self, the God of life; the God that is hurting at the dehumanisation of God's own creation. It is a cry and call to the Circle of Concerned African Women Theologians through its focus on Religion and Culture; to the people of God in our churches and other institutions in our society; to engage in study, research, theological reflection, and concrete actions, that will contribute to a better understanding of the impact of the global economic crisis on African women. It is a cry and call to convey the urgency and the centrality of engaging with economics (the present capitalist market-dominated ideology and its evils) as a matter of faith.

Two thirds of the countries that carry the debt burden are in Africa. Many of these have been forced into the implementation of structural adjustment programmes (SAPs) as a condition for debt reduction or debt cancellation. The emphasis on SAPs forces the so-called ailing economies to participate in the processes of neo-liberal economics; which is the basis of globalisation. This has resulted in an increasing number of the poor; growing unemployment and underemployment; reduction or stagnation of earnings; and diminishing access to education, health, housing and food security. A growing number of what would be productive human beings are excluded from meaningful participation in determining their livelihood, and in benefiting from the wealth of their countries. While disregarding the

---

[2] From Inter-Church Coalition on Africa, *Zambia: Still Shackled with Debt*, 1999, 2.

traditional boundaries of nation states, and the autonomy of nations and cultures, globalisation marginalises, excludes, socially disintegrates communities and has contributed to the increase of violence and civil conflict.

Fridah Muyale-Manenji has summed up the impact of globalisation in Africa as "a further undermining of the internal, national productive capacity, social security and democratic integrity of these (African) countries."[3]

The impact of the current economic policies on women's rights, and women's dignity has been critical, and therefore the focus of this address and the call Jubilee for African women. The poor of the world, and especially the majority of women, have been turned into slaves of the free market which has been elevated to a divine status beyond human control—with the declaration that there are no alternatives to the current trend. The market has been imbued with a divine status, with its own laws and disciplines, high priests (experts), and religious apologists for a distorted theology of sacrifice.[4] It is an economic system that is destroying African traditions, value systems and cultures, and is plundering the resources of the continent. It has set, not only Africa, but the whole world, on a collision course with the whole of creation.

What response and action is required to the critical economic injustice that has enslaved African women like Mama Chanda? Using the framework of jubilee and the themes of release from bondage, redistribution of wealth, and the renewal of the earth, I attempt to show how and why economic injustice caused by globalisaton hurts women in a different way from men; and why a call for jubilee needs to be attentive to the issues and concerns of women. We African women, owe it to the world and to ourselves to share the pain and

---

[3] Fridah Muyale-Manenji, "The Effects of Gloabalisation on Culture through the Eyes of an African Woman," in *Echoes* 12/1997 WCC Publication, 13.

[4] Jung Mo Sung, "Christian Faith and Globalisation," Issue Papers: Seeking the Common Good, United Church of Canada Moderator's Consultation, 1999.

suffering being experienced from the capitalist market-oriented system emanating from globalisation. We, African women have a unique responsibility to share what we know and think; and what we experience and the meaning of all this for our faith. Finally, we should boldly tell the world what we understand the gospel is calling us to do and to be.

The Concept of Jubilee

The concept of 'Jubilee' is at the centre of a world-wide movement that has inspired many reflections, writings and actions on how people can work together ecumenically through a global solidarity movement against the negative impact of the global capitalist market system. Jubilee has taken its strength from the Biblical vision of Jubilee as a call for a new beginning. Every seven years, Israel was to observe a Sabbath year marked by the cancellation of debts, the freeing of slaves and the rest of the land (Lev. 25; Deut. 15). The central value in the jubilee framework is the idea of conversion—"a fundamental reorientation of the heart and of society itself."[5] For Jesus, Jubilee was a permanent practice, as he declared at the start of his mission that God had sent him to proclaim release to the captives, recover sight for the blind, set at liberty those who are oppressed, and proclaim the acceptable year of the Lord (Lk. 4:18-19).

Recognising that over time, injustice and exploitation will enter into human relationships, and between human beings and the earth, Jubilee calls for a regular cycle of repentance, conversion, and renewal. Jubilee provides the mechanisms for righting broken relationships.

Notwithstanding some theological limitations that have been named by feminist theologians who have reflected on Jubilee as a framework for women's liberation, and the energy by women activists in the Jubilee 2000 movement in ensuring that there will be benefits for women should there be debt cancellation for the highly indebted countries, the jubilee framework has for me, the potential of

---

[5] Fr. Gerald Curry S.F.M., "So that you may live securely," in *A New Beginning: A Call for Jubilee*, Scarboro Foreign Missions Magazine Special Issue, 1998, 3.

enabling concerned individuals to stand in solidarity with the oppressed. It provides a moment for living out God's justice and has demonstrated the power of global solidarity on a focussed issue, in what has become popularly known as the Jubilee 2000 movement.

The central elements of this global movement in both the North and South is a recognition that the current global free market oriented economic system has increased poverty for the majority of the people in the South and has failed to promote human development. It is now estimated that sub-Saharan Africa owes over US$227 billion to creditors, about $400 for every man, woman, and child on the continent. Moreover, most of this debt was incurred by corrupt and oppressive governments, with full knowledge of this unhealthy situation by the lender governments and other financial institutions in the North. Now millions of people in Africa, the majority of whom are women and children, live in abject poverty while massive transfers of wealth go from their countries to the industrialised nations in the North. African governments are obliged by the IMF and other representatives of rich creditor nations to make unaffordable debt payments, neglecting the provision of basic needs such as health, education, clean water, sanitation, food security and other human development needs.

The global free market has eroded the power of nations to control, plan and regulate their own economies. This is evident through the imposition of SAPs, and the increasing power of multinationals vis-a-vis governments. Speaking at many forums, Archbishop Ndungane of South Africa has referred to this as 'the greatest scandal of our age.'

The urgent call is for a cancellation of international debt owed by the most highly indebted countries, (the majority of which are in Africa) and the establishment of a new economic order based on mutuality rather than exploitation. The urgent call is to give the poor nations a fresh start, a new beginning without any conditionalities.

Globalisation

Today, with or without our knowledge, we are all caught up in the enforced globalised capitalist market economy. Defined in a sophisticated way:

> Globalisation is the process of growing and intensifying inter-action at all levels of society in world trade, foreign investment and capital markets. It is abetted by technological advances in transport and communications and by the rapid liberalisation and deregulation of trade and capital flows, both nationally and internationally, leading to one global market.[6]

Globalisation is today one of the most significant forces affecting people world wide because of the accelerated pace of change—political, technological, environmental, social and cultural changes, economic changes and so forth, that are global, yet impacts the life of ordinary people at the very local level.

Commonly understood from what we all see and experience, globalisation is the emergence of a border-less free market in the world for the sole purposes of making the most profit out of any economic venture. I emphasise any economic venture because the quest for profit has no moral values any more.

For instance, the global market with its emphasis on competition with winners and losers, excludes millions of people from any meaningful participation in the economy. As corporations gain power over governments, governments have less ability to act on behalf of the people. For example, it no longer matters for our governments in Africa, to privatise industries with the knowledge that those men and women being laid off are the only breadwinners. By laying them off with no lasting benefits, they are being thrown into perpetual poverty. They and their dependants will lose access to food security, health, education, and in many cases, housing.

The main premise of globalisation is to get all countries in the world, regardless of their economic strength, to compete globally be-

---

[6] Rob van Drimmelen, *Faith in a Global Economy: A Primer for Christians*, (Geneva: WCC Publications, 1998), 7.

lieving that the quality of life will improve through the implementation of structural adjustment programmes, economic competitiveness, austerity programmes, shock therapy, and so forth. Free trade between countries brings economic benefits, and is the best way to bring about economic growth and improve living standards around the world.

Therefore, the debt crisis, high costs of social programmes, high taxes, trade barriers, national controls etc. are all barriers that must be removed to allow for the free market system to function. In the majority of African countries, the medicine to repair sick economies so that they can participate in the global market economy, has been the implementation of SAPs which has focussed on privatisation, trade liberalisation and deregulation.

In practice, austerity, shock therapy and SAPs have generally meant:

- Wide spread privatisation of state-owned enterprises
- Reductions in tax levels for corporations and the wealthy
- Cutbacks in social expenditure or what is referred to as fiscal discipline which include massive retrenchments of civil servants Removal of government price controls and subsidies
- Reduction in the level of tariffs and import quotas
- The promotion of export production
- The promotion of incentives to foreign investors such as tax holidays and free infrastructure
- Devaluation of local currency and moves toward labour market flexibility.

Supporters of the free market system point to increased economic growth, a decrease in inflation, and praise privatisation as a factor in attracting foreign investors. African governments are forever looking for buyers of their natural resources, land, minerals, water and so forth, with as few regulations as possible. They also argue that liberalisation of the economies has been a major factor in the increase of political freedom, and changes from dictatorship to electoral democracies.

If globalisation is so good, why are communities and especially women much poorer than ever before? Why is the gap between the rich and poor nations and persons within those nations getting wider and wider? The rich are getting richer and the poor are getting poorer. With such gaps in wealth, technology and knowledge, the playing field is not level, and therefore not free for fair competition of a free market.

Why do we have an urgent ecological crisis on our hands? Human wellbeing in the long run is dependent on healthy ecological system. Any economy that violates the ecological system for its own growth, needs or profit is doomed. Global warming and climate change, threats to life systems, forests, wetlands and coastal areas, are examples of the unsustainability of the economic system.

Why do we have so much armed conflict and civil strife in Africa? Poverty and environmental pressures have linkages to the increasing and profound societal violence and dysfunction in many developing countries. The war in Angola, Congo, etc. is more about gaining power over and control of resources than mere ethnic differences.

Why is there an over-consumption by few who have the financial resources and economic power and freedoms which have led to greed, exploitative systems of overproduction, marginalisation and exclusion of the majority who are forced to live on less and less? Surely we should all benefit from the blessings of globalisation equally?

Why is it that for the majority of the poor, despite the rhetoric of democratisation and popular participation, the experience is that of exclusion from meaningful participation in the economic and political lives of their nations and communities? Shifts of power and control from states to multinationals means that governments have lost the capacity to provide for the social needs of their citizens. We have seen in Africa the increase of violent repression as a response to challenge from civil society.

Why are lesser developed nations largely excluded from the global market place? For example, the whole of sub- Sahara Africa has less than 2% of the world trade.

The Impact on Women

The typical model of a woman in many African cultures is defined in relation to a man—that of a wife and mother, caring, submissive, obedient, respectful, hardworking, cooperative, one who endures all etc. An African woman's work at home remains unrecognized in economic terms. Admittedly some women have succeeded in being different from this model. They are protectors and providers, strong and daring, powerful and dynamic, competitive in spirit, their only obstacle being the patriarchal system which does not recognise their God-given capabilities. In spite of modern realities of our time, many women still live in a context where family, media, religion, politics, educational institutions and economic models, are all structured and operate in a way that limits women's potential and choices in life.

In order to gain a deeper understanding as to why women are differently impacted by economic injustice and other forms of oppression, we must understand the machinations and power embedded in the patriarchal system which perpetuates the model of the African woman described above. Patriarchy is a social system which supports and sanctions the predominance of men, giving men a concentration of power and privileges which are used in the subordination and oppression of women.

We need to seriously reflect and analyse gender roles that have become institutionalised in social practises and ideas which support power imbalances between men and women.

African women have suffered more from the impact of the economic crisis mainly because the thinking behind the macro-economic policies on which SAPs are based, while couched in gender-neutral language, takes little account of the sexual division of labour in households, and the strength of cultural oppression that exists. It is women who are making SAPs work, with their unpaid labour, they take over where the government has withdrawn, in health by looking after the sick, or through increased labour to earn money to pay those school fees. Women are performing two to three jobs at a time.

Because women are stretched to the limit, this is leading to the disintegration of family, household and community. In many instances, women have to deal with the tension between keeping the household together as they are expected by culture, and going out to earn money as the economy demands of them.

Globalisation has placed overwhelming pressure on subsistence economies where the majority of women are found. Loss of land, forest and water as well as access to these resources because of privatisation or sale to agribusiness, has driven many into destitution or into cities that have nothing better to offer. For some, the loss of traditional resource management capacity, such as living in balance with nature for long-term survival has meant that women are removed from nature. The loss of indigenous life skills that are critical for survival in subsistence economies leaves women devalued, excluded and marginalised. The survival of the fittest mentality of the competitive market economy takes away from women the community survival skills, by emphasizing private rights over community rights. Globalisation is not just an economic phenomena—it is as much political, philosophical and cultural value.

Women Living out Jubilee

The Circle of Concerned African Women Theologians has made great contributions in enabling and making visible the emerging expressions of African women's theology. A theology which is in solidarity with African women. A theology which has focussed on highlighting the struggles, contexts and situations in which African women of faith are challenged to live. The theology being expressed reflects anger, resentment, and bitterness on one hand, and on the other, hope, resilience and steadfast faith in a God of life. The analysis of women's realities have included themes of patriarchy, the impact of religion on African women's lives, critical examination of the power in myths and beliefs that keep women down, the oppressive nature of rituals of sexuality, marriage and family life including polygamy and monogamy, widowhood and singleness, motherhood and birthing, and so forth.

Through the All Africa Conference of Churches, the church women's movement brought to the attention of the African churches the issues of economic justice, child survival and especially that of the girl child, women's health, food security, women and the environment, and women in peace-making. For African women, theology is life, life as it is lived and experienced in community with others. African women are providing a vision of a community that lives as though God is indeed with us. Listening to Mercy Amba Oduyoye speaking on Jesus and the empowerment of women, Mercy affirms that what we read of the Jesus work with women, confirms that Jesus was a person of good news. The story of Jesus' encounter with women is good news because it is life-giving, liberative, and energising. The centrality of the value to love God and one's neighbour makes all God's creation accountable to each other. This is good news!

As we enter the new millennium, the situation of women is no better. We have seen increased poverty, suffering and death. We still live in a world that thrives on non-life giving economic systems and participate in a church that is largely silent on women's issue to the extent that in many of our contexts a life-giving theology for women is threatening to the status quo. The stones we talked about in 1988 at the start of the Ecumenical Decade Churches in Solidarity with Women are still there, they have just been shifted around. The barriers to participation are intact for many women. We were not surprised to hear that the experience of the Decade for many women in the church was that the Ecumenical Decade of Churches in Solidarity with Women turned out more to be the Ecumenical Decade of Women in Solidarity with Women. Women worked more on women's issues than the whole church did.

What will a jubilee for women look like? Who will roll the stone away? How shall we roll the stone away? These questions need answers. During the Ecumenical Decade Churches in Solidarity with

Women, solidarity was the defining framework for all actions, because we believed that solidarity would produce sustainable changes
in structures and transparent and progressive relationships among
women and men in church and society. We know that where as some
of these ideals may have been achieved in isolated situations, concrete
changes still have to come.

Much needs be done in ensuring economic justice for women, to
stop violence against women, and in removing barriers to women's
full participation in church and society. The impact of what we do in
addressing these issues calls for a church that is committed to work
in partnership with women. Partnership that calls for the involvement of all God's people in a mission for wholeness and mutual
empowerment through the employment of all gifts, and especially the
gifts that women bring into the partnership. This partnership calls for
mutual accountability, trust, honesty, forgiveness and persistent love.
The work we do must address systemic justice issues. This means
tackling the heart of institutionalised and organised social, cultural,
political and economic injustice. This struggle calls for continuous
challenge to power, so that the powerless can be empowered to
transform their own lives. Empowerment for women is about
women taking control of their own lives, addressing injustices, and
participating in the building of a more just world.

In the context of struggle for life, Mama Chanda's partnership
with God frees her to ask the hard questions and to name her poverty and exploitation as a sin. She knows her God as a God of life,
not death. As a woman of faith, she is aware that there are alternatives to the current economic system.

What she needs is a church that will move beyond its silence on
social justice issues and the passive participation in service-oriented
and charity roles, to a prophetic church that will participate with her
in the naming and denouncing the sin of structural injustice in church
and society.

Jubilee for women is a way of life. God calls us to love our
neighbour, and the jubilee is lived out when we do this in practice, to
live justice in our everyday lives. Jubilee emerges in a context of a
specific struggle, a struggle for life. The Bible has revealed several

stories of Jesus in solidarity with women which enables us make meaning of our own life struggles and experiences and we need to share what reading the Bible with new eyes has revealed to us as women.

Jubilee is liberative action, it cannot only be expressed as a vision. It must be acted out in all aspects of life by making connections between the struggle for economic justice and the cultural oppression of women, violence against women, and teachings of the church that reinforce certain behaviours in women.

The spirituality of Jubilee as has been demonstrated in the lives of African women is characterised by the spirit of resistance, resisting forces of death in all their various forms, resisting oppression, not just individual oppression, but that which we experience in common.

A jubilee for women must include strategies for survival that aim for structural changes in society, without which the struggle becomes a cycle.

At the close of the Decade in Harare, Musimbi Kanyoro challenged the churches to move beyond solidarity to accountability. Accountability means that we show the results of our solidarity with Mama Chanda. It is required of us. We must demonstrate in concrete ways what vision we bring to the challenges facing women so that we can make a contribution through study, research and actions which will

- enhance the understanding of the impact of economic injustice on African women;
- empower women in their search for survival strategies;
- enable theological reflection that will help communities make the connection between faith and economics;
- influence economic policy from a gender perspective;
- provide concrete tools and resources which can be used in deepening the understanding of economics as a matter of faith;
- call individuals and communities to engage in concrete liberative actions for women.

African women theologians must continue to articulate much more aggressively the African woman's theological insights and perspective on faith and economics. We have much to contribute to the transformation processes in our churches and communities in the next millennium. The search for wholeness, and the journey from brokenness to wholeness both individually and in community will only be realised when women's witness to Christ's ministry of love, justice and reconciliation is included.

We need to affirm and validate at all times, the strengths of African women like Mama Chanda, as demonstrated through her struggles for life and her resistance to the forces of death. We shall not cry, we must sing, dance and celebrate. Our God is able.

Keynote Address to the Circle for Concerned African Women Theologians, 10th Anniversary Celebrations—Accra, Ghana October 5-10, 1999.

Omega Bula is a Zambian Sociologist and Area Secretary for Southern Africa for the United Church of Canada Division of World Outreach.

10

Jubilaction: Engaging with a Feminist Jubilee in a Multi-faith and Secular Context

Denise Nadeau and Laurel Dykstra

Introduction

The biblical Jubilee is a program of periodic rest, release and redistribution of wealth. This ancient tradition has received new life as a vision of social change for the millennium. The Jubilee 2000 Campaign, aimed at pressuring the G8 nations to enforce cancellation of debts of the 50 poorest countries in the world, has brought an international profile to the vision of Jubilee.[1] Many mainline Christian churches have adopted Jubilee as a theme for church renewal. However, in the outpourings of theological reflections, campaigns, and bible studies, there has been little reference to the meaning or significance of Jubilee for women, especially poor women. This gap in the literature does not mean women are not engaging with Jubilee.[2]

This paper documents and analyses how a group of white, North American, feminist anti-poverty activists have popularised Jubilee in a multi-faith context. The Jubilee Action Group has created a play which documents the history of Jubilee in women's struggles for justice and freedom.

---

[1] In June 1999 the Jubilee 2000 Campaign presented a petition with 17 million signatures at the G8 Summit in Cologne. The results were disappointing with very little new money allocated for debt cancellation. The Southern countries have now taken the initiative with the campaign. With the slogan "Don't Owe, Won't Pay" they are urging southern governments to repudiate their debts and northern governments to reject Structural Adjustment Programs as a condition for debt cancellation.

[2] Connie Scott, "Jubilee: Radical Challenge and Promise Lev. 25," and "Jubilee: Visions and Strategies for Practical Hope Is 61, De 4:16-21," in *Envisioning A New Heaven and A New Earth* ed. Lalrinawmi Ralte, Florence Robinson, et al (Delhi: NCCI/ISPCK, 1998); Geraldine Smyth, "Sabbath and Jubilee" in *The Jubilee Challenge: Utopia or Possibility?* ed. Hans Ucko (Geneva:WCC Publications, 1997) 59-76; Carmelita M. Usog, "Sound the Trumpet for Justice, Liberty and Freedom," in *The Jubilee Challenge*, 188-195.

The Jubilee Action Group began in the spring of 1998 in the office of End Legislative Poverty in Vancouver British Columbia. We formed to use the Jubilee vision to fight economic injustice and impoverishment in BC, and to develop a feminist perspective on Jubilee. We were frustrated with the Jubilee 2000's campaign for its lack of feminist economic analysis, the single action focus on the petition, its omission of the issue of reparations and the glossing over of issues of impoverishment at home. In the context of the globalisation of capitalism, there is in Canada a growing polarisation between rich and poor. The middle class is shrinking while numbers of working poor, unemployed and homeless increase.[3] The Jubilee Action Group defined its mandate as promotion of the Jubilee vision beyond the churches in order to link Jubilee to local struggles for economic justice. We used Jubilee as a lens to view contemporary struggles against economic injustice.

The Jubilee Action Group consists of both women and men; its membership includes student, anti-poverty, labour movement and faith-based activists. We are not all Christians and the Christians in the group are social justice activists outside the church. We have two committees—the Women Against Poverty Committee and the Direct Action Committee. The Woman Against Poverty Committee has produced and performs the play *Jubilaction*. We, the authors, are members of this group.

We both come to this work from similar locations as theologically-trained Euro-Canadian activists working outside the institutional church. We work with different sectors of the marginalized and working poor in British Columbia. Denise works as a popular educator with unions that organise low-income service workers, as well as with women's and anti-poverty organisations. Laurel is a Catholic Worker and works with low-income seniors, residential hotel tenants and sex trade workers in the downtown core of Vancouver. We both wrestle with whether our faith is just a backdrop and grounding for

---

[3] The ratio of income of the richest 10% of Canadian families compared to the poorest 10% is 314 to one, a five-fold increase in the last 20 years. Women, children, people of colour and indigenous people are most impacted by this shift. "The Growing Gap," (Toronto: Centre for Social Justice, 1998), x.

our work or whether it can have prophetic and proclamatory relevance in a secular society. Despite these similarities, we approach this project quite differently: Laurel never questioning that the Levitical code is the logical place to begin, Denise adamant that the starting point is women's bodies and lives.

Which Jubilee and for Whom?

The critiques of Southern theologians, both of the Jubilee 2000 movement and the various Jubilee campaigns in the North provided us with some direction to make Jubilee relevant beyond a white middle class church constituency.

Tissa Balasuriya,[4] a Catholic Oblate priest from Sri Lanka, has challenged the Northern churches' narrow understanding of Jubilee as the cancellation of debts. For him, the fundamental issue is not what the South owes the North, but what the North owes the South after 500 years of colonialism and the recent neo-colonialism under capitalist globalisation. Cancellation of debts can only be effective if accompanied by redistribution of wealth and land globally. Balasuriya calls for restorative justice, restoration of stolen cultural artefacts and a rewriting of western theology and history to acknowledge the moral bankruptcy of colonialism and neo-colonialism.

A similar critique has been developed by the Pan African Healing Foundation, an organisation formed to provide a voice for Africans living in the UK and in the Diaspora. This group has critiqued the Jubilee 2000 campaign for perpetuating "the myth of the liberal white saviour" and for targeting debt while ignoring the root causes of the problems of Africa. It has also challenged the credibility of the churches and organisations like Christian Aid, which initiated Jubilee 2000, as believable spokespersons for Jubilee, because of their racist

---

[4] Tissa Balasuriya, "Theological Reflections on the Way to Jubilee," Call to Action Conference, Cassette recording, Detroit Michigan, November, 1998.

and colonial history. "When you carry a past without acknowledging it, everything you take on in the future is cast in doubt."[5]

Mercy Oduyoye, a feminist theologian from Ghana, provided us with a Southern feminist critique. Her comment on the Jubilee 2000 campaign was short and succinct: "It sounds like something for their kind of religion (the Northern churches); for me I work with what is around me, what I can change, what will help poor women in my community. All this talk of justice and world trade is just talk unless people actually do something."[6]

Balasuriya, Oduyoye and the Pan African Healing Foundation's challenges resonated with us. How could we present Jubilee as a vision of restorative justice that spoke to the root causes of impoverishment in Canada? How could we connect Jubilee to the colonial history of our country, and in particular the stealing of aboriginal land? What could make Jubilee a call to action, rather than what Don Pedro Casaldaliga, Roman Catholic Bishop of Sao Felix do Araguaia has called "jubilee **lite**—a celebration indifferent to the reality of the misery that surrounds us?"[7] Lastly, how could we connect Jubilee to the realities of the lives of poor women?

We were faced with the challenge of how to use a tradition rooted in Judaism and Christianity to organise against poverty and economic injustice in Vancouver BC, a city whose majority populations are non-Christian. Many of the poor in BC come from secular backgrounds or have been alienated from Christianity; many have roots in other faiths and traditions: Sikhism, Hinduism, Buddhism and First Nations' spiritualities. For native women and immigrant women from the South their experience with Christianity is so tied to colonialism and patriarchy that they have a deep distrust of the Bible. Many poor women from Christian backgrounds have had negative

---

[5] Excerpt from the UNESCO Slave Route Project Conference Document, The Pan African Healing Foundation, London, September 8, 1998.

[6] Mercy Oduyoye. Personal conversation with Denise at Bossy Ecumenical Institute in Geneva, Switzerland January, 1999.

[7] Don Pedro Casaldaliga, "El Cuerno Del Jubileo: Jubileo 2000," circular fraterna, January 1998, in *Jubileo Ano 2000*, CRIE, Mexico, July, 1998. Casaldaliga uses "jubilee light" in the Spanish text but we have modified it to "lite."

experiences with the dominant charity mode with which most churches relate to poor people. The long history in British Columbia of trade union militancy has provided many labour activists with a secular left framework that has equated most religion with fundamentalism. Within our own group, especially among the anti-poverty activists, there is a strong concern that if we seem 'too' Christian we will lose support and audiences.

We knew by the experience and make-up of our group that Jubilee had an appeal for secular and post-Christian feminists. We needed to transmit that appeal in a way that provided entry points for people not rooted in a Christian or Jewish faith-perspective but who also respected and did not dilute the core of the Jubilee program. We also wanted to present Jubilee in a way that connected and inspired audiences to action. The majority of us used popular education in our work so it made sense for us to turn to popular theatre as the vehicle for our message. If we embodied, enfleshed, the rather abstract principles of the Jubilee program in theatre perhaps Jubilee could come alive for those who knew little or nothing about it.

Feminist Popular Theatre: The Medium as Message

The term "popular theatre" refers to the many ways people from oppressed groups use theatre to educate and organise themselves and others. Popular theatre often links theatre with a particular experience and struggle. It can both empower the people involved in its creation and present a powerful political or social message. Often, as in our case, the actors are non-professionals involved in the particular struggles that the theatre points to or connects with.[8]

Feminist theatre, which can be both popular or professional, is based on these principles: "women's experience as primary, the celebration of the body in joy and suffering, unmasking the interconnections of racism-sexism-classism-homophobia, power-sharing and

---

[8] Rachel Epstein, Editorial, "Special Issue on Popular Theatre," *Participatory Research Newsletter*, Toronto, Spring 1987, 3.

mutuality, the reclamation of women's history, and community building as a goal."[9] The play, *Jubilaction,* combines these feminist theatre principles with the practice of popular theatre.

Unlike some forms of popular theatre which are based on the lived experience of characters in the present or recent past, *Jubilaction* uses historical characters to provide links with women's lives today. Inspired by an article of Peter Linebaugh—which traced the history of Jubilee in working class struggles on both side of the Atlantic during the 18th and 19th centuries—we tell stories of what Jubilee meant to women in different historical periods.[10] The play combines narration, women's voices and songs to trace women's Jubilee in tribal Israel, the early church, the English Revolution, the Chartist period, and the ante-bellum anti-slavery movements.[11] As we read women into Jubilee history, women's history read back to us a broader understanding of what Jubilee could mean.

Jubilaction is a form of feminist popular theatre that enacts feminist liberation theology, reinforcing the work of Victoria Rue, feminist theologian and playwright, who argues that feminist theatre must be a laboratory for feminist theology.[12] Our production of this feminist popular theatre has allowed us to develop both a feminist liberation hermeneutic and a deeper understanding of the sacred in women's resistance and rebellion against oppression. The play is an

---

[9] Victoria Rue, *"Cancerbodies:" Women Speaking the Unspeakable. Feminist Theatre Enacts Feminist Theology,* Unpublished Doctoral Thesis, Graduate Theological Union, 1994, 28, 223.

[10] Peter Linebaugh, "Jubilation: Or, How the Atlantic Working Class Used the Biblical Jubilee Against Capitalism, With Some Success" in *The New Enclosures,* Midnight Notes Collective (New York: Automedia, 1990), 84-97.

[11] While we have had requests from non-aboriginal people to put in a scene involving aboriginal women and Jubilee we decided not to. Jubilee represents a tradition in the religion that was used to colonize Native peoples and has not been taken up historically by Native women, to our knowledge. While Jubilee clearly speaks to the question of returning traditional tribal lands, it speaks to the colonizer.

[12] Victoria Rue argues that feminist theatre is not only necessary to feminist theology, "it is its essential laboratory." "A medicine show, a miracle play, street theatre—a place of storytelling and action—an arena that is inextricably linked to the radical liturgies and theologies we call feminist." Victoria Rue, Op. cit.

intersection of sacred texts—the canonical Jubilee texts, and the sacred texts of women's lives, past and present. By analysing examples from the play where our many texts intersect we will explore the unique aspects of our developing hermeneutics, and then assess how the combination of our hermeneutics with our feminist popular theatre methodology allows us to transmit the particular vision of Jubilee to specific non-Christian audiences.

The Biblical Jubilee

Throughout the development of the play, we became increasingly aware of our regard for all of our sources as sacred scripture. Although our understanding of sacred scripture is by no means limited to traditional canon, the biblical Jubilee was a starting point for some members of the group. Based on our reading, our research and our developing understanding of the pervasiveness and possibility of Jubilee, our definition of biblical Jubilee texts is very broad.

Leviticus 25 and *Deuteronomy 15* outline two periodic remission programs which together include debt cancellation, return of tribal land, release and restoration of slaves and bond-servants and rest for all. This Priestly law and Deuteronomistic exhortation are the Jubilee texts most often cited. Because the Lukan author chose Isaiah 61:1-7, the "Year of the Lord" speech, to inaugurate Jesus' public ministry as "jubilee practitioner"[13] (Lk 4:15-21) these are the best known Jubilee texts from the Prophets and the Christian Bible. Yet the demands of the Jubilee program—renew the earth, liberate slaves, cancel debts, redistribute wealth—pervade the sacred texts of the Christian and Jewish traditions beyond these familiar examples. These demands are part of a broad pattern of Sabbath economics which emphasizes justice and abundance but puts limits on accumulation.[14]

---

[13] Ched Myers, "Jesus' New Economy of Grace," *Sojourners* 27(4) 1998, 36-39, 38.

[14] For a comprehensive review of Sabbath economics see Ched Myers, "God Speed the Year of Jubilee! The Biblical Vision of Sabbath Economics," *Sojourners* 27 (3,4) 1998, 24-39; 36-39.

The pervasiveness and rhythmic quality of Sabbath economics: seventh day, seventh month,[15] seventh year and Jubilee: *seven times seven plus one*, are amplified by multiple references and traditions. In Exodus 16 the economy of abundance is profoundly illustrated when former slaves eat bread from heaven for free and celebrate a day of rest. Exodus 20:8-11; 23:10-12 and Deuteronomy 5:12-15 command the seventh day and year to be set aside for the rest of all: land, animals, workers, slaves and aliens. These commands are grounded in the memory of Egyptian slavery. In the *Book of Ruth*, a destitute, foreign widow has the right to rest and dignified work freely chosen.[16]

The Prophets rail against the betrayal of the Jubilee program therby nuancing it further: Isaiah promises desolation for those who accumulate land, joining house to house and adding field to field (5:8); Amos denounces neglect of those who glean "selling the sweepings of the wheat" (8:6) and Micah identifies with the landless decrying violent land seizure (2:2). Jeremiah's "poetics of denunciation"[17] credit the destruction of Jerusalem and the Babylonian exile to Israel's failure to live as Sabbath people. Accompanying these calls for Jubilee renewal is a scathing rejection of piety without justice.

In these texts and others the dangerous memory of the historical Jubilee echoes and re-echoes. But along with the record of this subversive practice are preserved unquestioned oppressive practices particularly with respect to women. The biblical Jubilee does not sanction rest from reproductive labour, does not question the institution of slavery nor violence against women and does not acknowledge any but male Israelites as full persons, entitled to Jubilee's full abundance. More subtle but at least as problematic, the prophetic literature's radical denunciation of Israel's slide into the economics of accumulation is inseparable from polemical tirades against neighbouring religions and a repeated, extended metaphor of Israel as whoring bride and YHWH as scorned husband. This metaphor presents Israel's

---

[15] Arthur Waskow, "Beyond Marx and Buddha: The Jubilee" in *Wrestling With God*, 1978, 117.

[16] Arthur Waskow, "Holy Economics: A Rhythm of Worthy Work and Reflective Rest," *Sojourners* 26(5) 1997, 34-36.

[17] Linebaugh, op. cit. 86.

commitment to redistributive economics in terms of a woman's fidelity to a marriage (property) contract and images the divine in the classic pattern of an abusive partner, alternating between assault and gentle attentiveness. For women who in whatever time or culture are at some level enslaved by the economic control or the physical violence of a male partner, where is their Jubilee? And why should people of other faiths consider an economic program which appears neither to respect nor include them?

In the Christian Scriptures certain demands for Jubilee practice are resurrected. Although the Jesus movement broadened and inclusivised the Jubilee vision in some respects, they diminished it in others, food is emphasised and land de-emphasised. The Jubilee theme pervades a scripture, the Bible, that throughout history and into the present has been used with malice and with good intention against those whom Jubilee privileges: the impoverished, the enslaved, the landless—workers and women.

In our work the Jubilee Action Group is not limited by the patriarchal, violence and slavery-accepting aspects of the biblical Jubilee texts, but neither do we ignore nor defend them. Biblical texts have both preserved and distorted the stories of women. Our play writes women back into the history of Jubilee in three biblical time periods: tribal Israel, post-exilic Jerusalem and early Jesus movement. To do so we draw on the above texts, historical research, particularly historical Jesus scholarship and the recent out-pouring of Jubilee writing. But we draw just as strongly on our own feminist biblical imaginations and knowledge of our own lives and bodies as we work, rest, love, struggle and play.

The scene from tribal Israel most clearly illustrates this intersection of scholarship and biblical imagination. Three generations of women articulate the Levitical Jubilee program.[18] Because there are

---

18 This scene and at some level the style of the play were influenced by Elen Frankel's *The Five Books of Miriam, A Woman's Commentary on the Torah*, (San Francisco: HarperSanFrancisco, 1998). We were delighted with Frankel's interplay of different women's voices and perspectives.

so few biblical women and so many of those we know of are un-named, we consider it an important aspect of feminist recovery work to speak women's names. In the first scene Havah, Devorah and De-vorah's mother Miriam lay out the four demands which the Jubilee Action Group has identified: renew the earth, cancel debts, redistrib-ute wealth, liberate slaves.[19] They assess how these demands meet and fail to meet their needs in situations of wealth, debt-slavery, pa-triarchal family economics and domestic/reproductive labour. Rather than describe the scene we will let the women speak for themselves.[20]

Scene 1
(Devorah is on stage fixing her scarf and preening)

(Enter Havah, excitedly)

H: Devorah, Devorah…. have you heard about this Jubilee? Its a law that says every 50 years land is returned to the people who had it first, debts are cancelled and slaves are set free!

D: I've never heard of that; that's garbage

H: It is not… my grandmother told me. You just think it's garbage because you're so spoiled you couldn't live without me as your slave.

D: What do you mean? You're not my slave? You're my friend (throws her scarf aside).

H: Yeah right, a friend who gets you up in the morning, brushes your hair, washes your clothes, picks up after you (retrieving and folding Devorah's scarf).

D: Well… (Sputter, sputter)

H: Besides, Jubilee is about more than just slaves; it means you'll have to give the land you own back to the people who had it first.

D: But it's ours (stamping her foot, raising her voice).

Miriam (entering): Devorah, Havah, what's going on in there? I can hear you from the other room.

---

[19] As we perform these demands are displayed on banners around the performance space so that Jubilee is presented through specific examples and general principles.

[20] The scenes we have created for the biblical time periods are ironically the most "Jubilee-based" in that they focus specifically on the biblical texts. At the same time they are the least "historically accurate" of our scenes as we do not include named and verified women from history as we do with later time periods.

D: Mother, Havah's talking about some stupid Jubilee thing that no one's ever heard of.

H: People have too heard of it, my grandmother told me.

M: Actually Devorah, Havah is right, you know about the Sabbath? Every seventh day and seventh year is a time of rest and renewal...well Jubilee is the 7x7th year. The 50th year is also a time of rest, renewal and redistribution for people and for the land.

D: How come I've never heard of this before?

H: Why would you pay attention to anything that's good news for slaves?

M: Don't you remember when you were ten, it was a Sabbath year and we didn't work the land and your father cancelled debts?

D: No.

H: That's because the fathers and brothers and husbands rest while women continue to work in the home, make food and raise the children....everyone you knew was still working.

D: But is it true that Havah goes home and I have to do everything by myself? Can't we just get a foreign slave?

M: Well, Hebrew slaves are released...

H: And that's not all, my grandmother told me we get some of your flocks and grapes and wheat and land so that we have enough to start over and my family won't have to be slaves again.

D: Well you won't, what would you do with sheep and wheat? You can't own land, you're a girl.

M: Everybody's supposed to get what they need to survive.

H: If that happens, we're going to be poor, we'll lose our land...

M: The truth is Devorah, the land we live on doesn't really belong to your father, it belongs to the Creator and Jubilee means that nobody is poor or rich forever, everybody gets what they need (the three players freeze).

Sacred Scriptures

We locate this paper within the recent movement to define feminist interpretation as something other than a biblical project. [21] The Bible has not only been used to oppress women, but it has been used as the justification for slavery, colonisation and genocide. If sacred scripture is defined only as the Bible or as written texts, women's voices and stories are left out; the richness of the scriptures from other traditions are lost and non-written forms—oracles, performances, storytelling and dances—are excluded.[22]

Feminist liberation theologians from many continents are redefining what sacred scriptures mean to them. In Asia women are including in their scriptures texts from Buddhism, Hinduism and Taoism; African women are telling the myths and stories orally transmitted through ancestors; in North America womanists have defined the slave narratives as sacred texts and both in Latin America and North America Spanish-speaking women are defining women's lives as sacred texts.[23]

This transgression of scriptural boundaries is based on women reclaiming the power to name—to name what is sacred, what is the revelation of God and where that revelation takes place. "Authority is no longer within texts, rather it is measured by the liberation of women and all God's oppressed people of the world."[24] In the context of oppression women witness to God in naming what is healing, liberating or sustaining for them.

Musa W. Dube Shomanah uses the term "oral-Spirit" as a framework to describe women's sacred scriptures in post-colonial

---

[21] Elisabeth Schussler Fiorenza, "Introduction," in *Concilium 1998/3: Women's Sacred Scriptures*, eds. Kwok Pui-lan and Elisabeth Schussler Fiorenza (Orbis: Maryknoll, New York, 1998), 1.

[22] Kwok Pui-lan, " Reflections on Women's Sacred Scriptures," in *Women's Sacred Scriptures*, Ibid. 105.

[23] Elisabeth Schussler Firenza, "Introduction," op.cit. 3; Joan M. Martin, "The Slave Narratives and Womanist Ethics," in *Women's Sacred Scriptures*, 65-73 inspired our reading of the spirituals.

[24] Dube Shomanah, Musa W, "Scripture, Feminism and Post-Colonial Contexts," in *Concilium* 1998/3: *Women's Sacred Scriptures*, 47.

contexts. "Oral" refers to women's history and unrecorded words. She uses the term "Spirit" because it "recognizes divine partnership."[25] For us the term oral-Spirit also affirms women as Body/Spirits, a unity from which women speak "their own sacred, life-affirming and liberating words of wisdom."[26] In producing and performing *Jubilaction* we are taking up Dube Shomanah's challenge to feminists to move beyond re-reading ancient patriarchal and colonizing scriptures and to "rewrite, create, hear, speak, sense and feel new sacred words of life, wisdom, liberation and justice."[27] We recover the suppressed scriptures of women who interpreted the Jubilee tradition in their own times and from their locations as oppressed working class and slave women struggling for liberation. In doing so they stood over and against patriarchy, capitalism and imperialism.

For our exploration of the Jubilee tradition in recent times, we used the resources available to us: journals, history books, novels, song collections, and pamphlets. Many of these sources and resources reveal sites where women's participation in struggle is both recorded and obscured. So, like biblical texts we approach them with suspicion, interrogating for evidence of the women we know are there. We found allies in various disciplines: Stevie Davies has written history of women radicals of the English Revolution,[28] Dorothy Thompson documents women's involvement in the Chartist movement[29] and in her book *Jubilee*, Margaret Walker tells the story of a slave woman in Georgia.[30] These women historians and novelists pointed us towards women's Jubilee scriptures.

---

[25] Dube Shomanah, ibid. 52, 53.

[26] *Ibid.* 53.

[27] *Ibid.*

[28] Stevie Davies, *Unbridled Spirits: Women of the English Revolution, 1640-1660.* (London: The Women's Press, 1998).

[29] Dorothy Thompson, *Outsiders: Class, Gender and Nation*, (London: Verso Press, 1993).

[30] Margaret Walker, *Jubilee*, (New York: Bantam, 1966).

Jubilee songs provided a different kind of scripture for the play. Songs from specific eras offered insights into how Jubilee was understood at that time and how it fit with other contemporary ideas. Thomas Spence's 1782 "Jubilee Hymn: Or A Song to be Sung at the Commencement of the Millennium, If Not Sooner"[31] is focused on landlords and rent capitalism. Numerous spirituals, often the province and product of enslaved women,[32] communicate the joy of emancipation and condemn slavery.

> This is the day of Jubilee
> God's gonna build up Zion's walls
> Lord has set the people free
> God's gonna build up Zion's walls[33]

Jubilaction is an intersection of sacred scriptures. Biblical, historical and fictional women speak their own words, anonymous words, words of the bible, words of their male contemporaries and words of the Jubilee Action Group. Our decisions about which voices to privilege, which strands to follow and how to combine texts were made easily, not based on church sanction, historicity or external authority but on the texts' capacity to communicate women's struggles for justice and freedom. In measuring sacred scriptures' authority by the extent to which it calls us to liberation from oppression and from being oppressors we maintain the understanding of scripture as a tradition which calls us up short, which challenges us to what we are not. Implicit in our group's work is the understanding that public words, no matter who speaks or writes them, are at some level collective products. Our writing does not add women where they were absent; rather, it restores them where they had been erased and silenced.

---

[31] Linebaugh, op. cit. 85.

[32] Lisa Pertillar Brevard. "'Will the Circle Be Unbroken' African-American Women's Spirituality in Sacred Song Traditions," in *My Soul Is a Witness* Gloria Wade-Gayles, 32-47, 33.

[33] This spiritual which speaks of the day of emancipation became the basis for the North American labour song, "Great Day." Instead of God building Zion's walls, "We're gonna build our union strong."

Intersecting Texts

The play tells Jubilee as women's history of resistance, especially to economic oppression, by presenting scenes, narrative commentary and song from different historical periods where women acted on the vision of Jubilee. The two scenes we present next come from specific European historical contexts yet they appeal to diverse audiences.

During the English Revolution, when common lands were enclosed and tenant farmers evicted from their holdings, various resistance groups—Levellers, Quakers, Fifth Monarchists and Separatists—offered religious and political solutions. The True Levellers or the Diggers proposed economic solutions as well: an end to clearing forests on the commons, distribution of Church and Royalist land to the poor and free access of all to the commons. In 1649, they tore down fences on St. George's Hill, Surrey and established the first of several non-violent farming communities on common land outside of London. The Diggers and Levellers, without ever using the word Jubilee, were a movement based in Jubilee principles: redistribution of wealth through land, the primary claim of poverty and hunger over luxury and accumulation, scorn for religion/piety which did not benefit the poor, communal wealth/ownership, food as fundamental and land as sacred.

We present this Jubilee history through Leveller Katharine Chidley, an historical figure and leafleter of the time. Katharine Chidley speaks in her own words and the words of a anonymous Leveller's pamphlet, quite likely the work of women printers and leafleters:

> Oh that the cravings of our stomachs could be heard by the Parliament and City! Oh that the tears of our poor famished babes were bottled! Oh that their tender mothers' cries for bread to feed them were engraven in brass...

Oh Parliament men and soldiers! Necessity dissolves all laws and government, and hunger will break through stone walls; tender mothers will sooner devour you, than the fruit of their own womb.[34]

Behind her, mute players sculpt their bodies first into a tableau that depicts women's struggling to survive, picking roots, holding an empty food basket, cradling a crying baby. In a second tableau, as Katherine heaps scorn on the clerics and lords of the land the players raise fists to show their resistance to oppression. When a narrator tells of other revolutionary women, Katharine Chidley is surrounded by a group of her contemporaries, calling out their names—*Mary Carey, Lucy Hutchinson, Anna Trapnel, Mary Fisher.*[35] As Katherine lists the violent responses which women's actions drew from those in power, *we were whipped, stocked or carted off to prison,* the players drop to the ground in turn. Then one by one the women rise and proclaim in their continued resistance the words of Digger spokesperson Gerard Winstanley and other male revolutionaries.[36]

The Katharine Chidley scene is our most complex in terms of its internal intertextuality. Here is one example. Katharine Chidley's first speech comes from an anonymous Leveller's pamphlet which speaks about women's experience from the authority of suffering bodies.[37] The Leveller authors, in 1648 used the words of 8th Century BCE prophets Amos and Micah to denounce the disparity between England's rich and poor.

Oh you Members of Parliament and rich men in the city, that are at ease and drink wine in bowls and stretch yourselves on

---

[34] 1648 Leveller's pamphlet , Stevie Davies, op.cit. 71.

[35] These are the names of actual women of the English Revolution. Stevie Davies, op. cit.

[36] There are actually five sources, broadsheets, and speeches making up the chorus of revolutionary voices in this scene. Christopher Hill, *The World Turned Upside Down*, (London: Penguin, 1972).

[37] We know that Leveller women were involved in writing, printing and distributing pamphlets. Stevie Davies, op.cit. 70.

beds of down, you that grind our faces and flay off our skins...Is there none to pity?[38]

Amos 6:1	Alas for those who are at ease in Zion,
Amos 6:6	who drink from bowls
Amos 6:4	Alas for those who lie on beds of ivory and lounge on their couches,
Amos 2:7	they who trample the head of the poor into the dust of the earth
Micah 3:2	who tear the skin off my people and the flesh off their bones; who eat the flesh of my people, flay their skin off them.

These prophetic Jubilee texts provided a tradition and authority through which poor women could articulate the keenness of their want and their rage at social inequity. All of the above texts promise retribution, downfall and destruction for the rich. By adopting them these revolutionary women threaten those "who are at ease" in their day with a vision of Jubilee.

> You poor take courage
> You rich take care
> This earth was made a common treasury
> For everyone to share

These lines come from "The World Turned Upside Down"[39] and are based on the words of Winstanley. At the end of the scene we call the audience to stand and join us singing the tenets of the Digger movement and in that moment the texts of all our lives meet the texts of thirty centuries.

The Chartist scene was developed to illustrate the role of Jubilee in the history of the labour movement. We uncovered stories,

---

[38] Ibid. 71.

[39] *The Hospital Employees' Union Songbook*, (Vancouver: HEU, 1991), 89.

speeches and pamphlets of many women who were active in the Chartist resistance to the industrial revolution in the 1830's and 40's in Britain. The scene is a monologue by Elizabeth Hansen, a member of the Elland Female Anti-Poor Law Association in Yorkshire. Like many female radicals of the period she spoke at women-only meetings, where hundreds of women turned out. Women were a major force in the Chartist movement and formed their own organisations—the Female Chartist Associations. They joined in protests, riots and action against the hypocrisy of the established church, the exploitation of the employers and the encroachments of the state on the poor.[40] They based their grievances on appeals to natural rights and the Bible.

Elizabeth's monologue includes words from one of her speeches, a description of some of the organizing and demands of the Elland women, references from a Female Chartists' pamphlet and some of the words of William Benbow.[41] Benbow's proposal for the first general strike, the Grand National Holiday, was endorsed by the Chartist National Convention in 1839, and was based on Jubilee. For women like Hansen, forced to work in the factories and mines, often with their children, this call to rest had great appeal. In the play, as she describes the conditions of her life, four women behind her silently repeat the gestures of working at the power loom—one of the machines that had contributed to breaking up the family home craft work.

As she speaks the four workers in the back gradually slow down, come to a position of rest, then turn to face the audience. She steps back and joins them saying: *This month will be a festival for us and we know such a festival is approved by God. Thomas Benbow says it was an estab-*

---

[40] Dorothy Thompson, "Women and 19th Century Radical Politics—A Lost Dimension" in *Outsiders*, 131.

[41] Benbow was a radical pamphleteer who proposed the Grand National Holiday, one of the first conceptions of the general strike. It was based on the Levitical Jubilee. Dorothy Thompson, *The Early Chartists*, (London: Macmillan, 1971); Jutta Schwarzkopf, *Women in the Chartist Movement*, (London: Macmillan, 1991); William Benbow, "Grand National Holiday and Congress of the Productive Classes," ed. SEA. Bushnell, (London: Pelagian Press, no date).

lished custom among the ancient Hebrews, called the Jubilee. A holiday means a holy day, and ours is to be the most holy. Our holy day is to establish plenty, to abolish want, to render all equal.[42]

In embodying the Chartist women this way we present the women's Chartist Jubilee as resistance to wage slavery and relentless alienating work. We affirm the women's militancy, their solidarity with other groups, their level of organisation and the joy and fun they had working together. They were subverting the capitalist system by demanding that they had a right to be in the home and not have to sell their bodies and souls to a factory master for a starvation wage. In our bodies as performers we reiterate one of the core messages of Jubilee—the call to rest from all forms of slavery, to rest from agricultural labour, and to have a time where God and the justice of God are recognized as primary.

Our Working Hermeneutics

In any reading of scripture, however rigidly scripture is defined, the reader moves between texts and times, layers of redaction and intertextuality. This is especially true for the Jubilee Action Group in our work promoting "Sabbath Literacy."[43] In bringing the language and inspiration of Jubilee's redistributive economics to existing struggles, we draw from a diverse and unorthodox collection of scriptures. We transgress the unsettled boundaries of canon with eyes and hearts open—an ongoing act of "creative disobedience."[44] To the biblical texts we bring the texts of our lives, the lives of women in history and the lives of women who experience the play. In these texts "the non-biblical cultural texts bring out the hidden or neglected motifs of the biblical text."[45]

---

[42] Benbow, *op. cit.* 9.

[43] Myers, "Jesus' New Economy," 39.

[44] Dorothee Soelle, *Creative Disobedience*, (Cleveland: The Pilgrim Press, 1995).

[45] Archie Lee, "Cross Textual Hermeneutics on Gospel and Culture," *Asian Journal of* Theology 10(1) 1996, 38-48; 41.

In examining our *cross textual hermeneutics*[46] for this paper, it became clear that we were operating on two levels. We were deliberately employing some hermeneutical models as a conscious methodology, for example Gutierrez's hermeneutics of suspicion and Elisabeth Schussler Fiorenza's hermeneutics of feminist re-membering. At the same time we found another hermeneutics emerging naturally from our embodied engagement with the many texts. In the following pages we will name and explore three of the less formulaic ways that we have come to know the Scriptures: class analysis, reading through the body and collective engagement/action. It is through these three perspectives that we engage pluralistic audiences.

Class: Jubilee and Women's Struggles against Injustice

How we read Jubilee—the canonical texts, the Jubilee moments in women's histories and Jubilee in our own lives—is shaped by our own class location, identities and alliances. Of the six core members of our Jubilee Action Group all are white and either lesbian or bisexual. Four are working class; the two of us who are middle class work with and have made our alliances with poor and working class women and men. What is common to us, whether we come from a Christian, labour left, feminist, anti-racist or anti-poverty perspective-or all of the above—is that we share a radical critique of capitalism based on a class, race and gender analysis.

We bring to Jubilee a feminist political economy framework "rooted in an analysis of the changes in the material conditions of women's lives, as they have been affected by the restructuring of the world economy and the international division of labour."[47] This means that we are not only concerned about sexual and physical violence against women, but we also consider the structural violence of the economic policies of neo-liberal capitalism that have left millions

---

[46] Ibid

[47] Sylvia Federici, "Reproduction and Feminist Struggle in the New International Division of Labour," in Dalla Costa, Maria Rosa and G. Dalla Costa, eds. *Women, Development and the Labour of Reproduction: Issues of Struggles and Movements.* Lawrenceville, NJ.: Africa World Press, 1998, 2.

of women, children and men starving and/or dying slowly from poverty and exploitation of their labour.

Working class and poor women's work has been restructured under global capitalism. "It is no longer possible to look at issues of women's poverty in the North without considering how the restructuring of the world economy is responsible for not only the global spread of poverty, but also for the emergence of a new colonial order that deepens the divisions among women."[48] Women continue to work in factories, maquilas, and as landless peasants or agricultural workers. We continue to do much of the mostly unwaged reproductive labour, of producing and maintaining workers for capital, as teachers, nurses, healers, mothers, cooks, cleaners, sex workers, etc. This labour is clearly divided on class and race lines. The "new" international division of labour represents a gradual redistribution of women's reproductive labour on a North/South basis. Increasing numbers of Third World women are involved in servicing the reproductive needs of the North. These services include: working as domestics and home support workers, providing babies for adoption and the traffic in children, surrogate motherhood, working in the sex-tourist industry, becoming mail-order brides, and working as cheap domestic labour in the global tourist industry.

The traditional definition of working class—a male industrial labour force—no longer applies. Our definition of workers includes women migrant workers and domestics, indentured labourers, sex trade workers, homeworkers, the unemployed, refugees and recent immigrants. Beyond that our definition includes members of the most impoverished classes—single parents on welfare and all those on social assistance (in countries with social welfare), the homeless, members of communities marginalized by racism, and the mentally and physically disabled. Within the Canadian class structure the majority of aboriginal peoples continue to be the most impoverished race/class. This is the legacy of our country's history of colonization

---

[48] Sylvia Federici, *op. cit.* 1.

where Europeans conquered, plundered, stole the land, killed and enslaved the aboriginal peoples they encountered. The present neo-colonial structure which divides status and non-status Indians, Inuit and Metis, also serves to place aboriginal women at great disadvantage in terms of both property rights and protection from violence.[49]

How does this analysis shape our reading of Jubilee? Peter Linebaugh presents three Jubilee traditions in modern Western history— the aristocratic Jubilee, the bourgeois Jubilee and the proletarian Jubilee.[50]

> The working class experience with Jubilee is closer to home than the words and deeds of an illegitimate carpenter's son upon the periphery of the Roman Empire one thousand nine hundred and ninety years ago. We can find in the working class resistance to the history of mercilessness, both a scripture and a hermeneutics.[51]

Linebaugh argues that the biblical Jubilee tradition was an expression of anti-imperialism—opposing slavery, landlordship, credit and debit, the work ethic, and pollution of the earth. For thousands of years this meaning was distorted or ignored. "With the advent of industrial capitalism the enclosed working class of England and the enslaved African American working class rediscovered Jubilee. They adopted Jubilee to freedom and anti-capitalism; they expanded its meaning and gave it bite."[52]

We agree with Linebaugh's anti-imperialist analysis of Jubilee and that there was a proletarian/working class tradition of Jubilee.

---

[49] Howard Adams, *A Tortured People: The Politics of Colonisation*, Theytus Books, Penticton, BC, 1995, 11.

[50] The aristocratic tradition celebrated the 50th anniversary of monarchs, provided jubilee doors in the Vatican and supported the sale of jubilee indulgences for release from spiritual slavery. The bourgeois tradition tended to define jubilee as utopian and impractical, suggested reformist demands—eg. release of French prisoners-of- war, and focused on spiritual renewal. The proletarian tradition interpreted the Jubilee as liberation from capitalism and imperialism, as a program. Linebaugh, op.cit. 85.

[51] Linebaugh, ibid. 87.

[52] Linebaugh, ibid. 97.

We bring to his analysis and to the Jubilee texts our understanding of women as social and economic actors and agents of resistance to colonial and capitalist exploitation. Jubilee has had particular meanings for different groups of impoverished and exploited women throughout history.

Women have always been part of Jubilee, especially in the history of working class and slave struggles. But their stories and experiences are largely absent in the dominant discourse and in the biblical Jubilee texts. We uncovered voices of women that connect to the reality of working class women's lives today—migrant domestic workers, factory workers, women forced into workfare, mothers whose children are hungry.

Our reading of Jubilee was evidenced in our writing and performing the play. We recovered particular strands of our radical history as women of European descent. Yet we faced the challenge of making *Jubilaction* relevant beyond the particularity of white working class women's struggles. As white women we are heirs to a legacy of white supremacy and colonialism and we have an obligation to speak about racism as part of our analysis of Jubilee. We chose to present the story of women's resistance to slavery through songs and spirituals that incorporated the Jubilee vision rather than have white women represent black women. At the same time we reinforced the narrative of the play to represent and critique the ongoing racism, white supremacy and neo-colonial structures that we ourselves are part of.

In reading Jubilee from our feminist anti-imperialist perspective we find Jubilee in women's resistance to impoverishment, injustice and to old and new forms of slavery. Our starting point is not the repression or oppression of women, but how women have organised, resisted, and provided inspiration and hope for a more just world. In associating Jubilee with working class women's struggles we frame Jubilee as a vision and mobilising force for insurrection, for challenging the status quo.

Reading Jubilee from the Body

Women live and act in history through their bodies. Because women perform most of the reproductive labour in society their bodies are inscribed by that daily reality. Chung Hyun Kyung, in writing Asian women's theology, speaks of the epistemology of the broken body:

> Women's bodies are the most sensitive receivers for historical reality. Their bodies record what has happened in their lives. Their bodies remember what it is like to be no-body, and what it is like to be some-body.[53]

Women's bodies, which store the memories and stories of our lives, record the sacred in witnessing to joy, pleasure, survival, birth, resistance and well-being. Our bodies are witness also to violence and discrimination, to the absence of God. Women's experience as body has enabled us to challenge the androcentric and patriarchal texts that have ignored or violated women's bodies.

The naming and reading of women's lives and bodies as sacred texts is a recent development in feminist theology.[54] Reading from women's bodies as sacred texts challenges the patriarchal construct that God is above and outside the body. The divine is revealed in women's experiences of sexual ecstasy, giving birth and healing. The sacred becomes visible in the mundane daily life of the body.

The patriarchal split between soul and body, the sacred and the profane, is an essential construct of elite religion (religion practised by the elite classes) but it is not necessarily part of popular religiosity—which is and has been the territory of poor and indigenous women. Popular religiosity refers to the religious understandings, beliefs, rituals and practices of the masses. The experience of the sacred in the ordinary and of the spirit in the body, is very much part of women's popular religiosity. Its practice includes "concerns for daily experience such as healing the sick, finding lost objects, establishing

---

[53] Chung Hyun Kyung, in Rue, Ibid 55.

[54] Elsa Tamez, "Women's Lives as Sacred Text," in *Women's Sacred Scriptures*, Victoria Rue, "Cancerbodies."

desired relationships with other humans or animals, getting the crops to grow, safely delivering health babies, and properly preparing the dead for their departure from earth."[55] Working class and poor women responded to Jubilee out of a popular religiosity based in their struggle for daily survival.

Jubilee had meaning for women who were struggling for justice and freedom connected to their very embodied experiences of oppression—hunger; watching their children starve or be taken away; 14-16 hour days at back-breaking labour; physical, sexual and emotional violence, etc. Jubilee did not represent an abstract economic formula; rather women interpreted it in relation to the pains, sufferings, joys and dreams of their everyday lives. The initial Jubilee program—freeing slaves, resting the land, cancelling debts and redistributing wealth and land—affected women's bodies at many levels. It also ignored other dimensions of women's bodies. Our task has been to trace both the omissions and the instances where women's struggles gave new meaning to the program, as women witnessed to what justice, dignity and integrity for the body meant for them and their children.

We agree with Elsa Talmez that "not all of women's lives is sacred text; nor are the lives of all women," there are moments of discrimination, hatred or dominance exercised by women. Many biblical texts have functioned to promote and perpetuate violence against women. In recovering women's lives as sacred texts outside the canon we assess whether our use of the texts of women's lives will be harmful for or will help women's liberation. Our bottom line is to promote a vision that defends the sacrality and dignity of women's bodies.

---

[55] Paula Cooey, "Popular Religiosity," *Dictionary of Feminist Theologies*, eds. Letty M. Russell and J. Shannon Clarkson, (Louisville,Westminister John Knox, 1996), 214.

Collective Engagement/Action

But the interpretation of Holy Scripture does not find expression only in preaching and doctrine, and certainly not primarily in commentaries, but also in doing and suffering.[56]

Two critical aspects of how the Jubilee Action Group has come to understand Jubilee are testified to in our name. We are an *action group* and this is fundamental to how we know Jubilee, how we engage texts. Our readings of Jubilee are collective/community readings. As we illustrated in the previous section, it is possible to read the body as text; however it is possible for such "body readings" to be privatized and individualistic. Such personalized readings are quite distant from our Jubilee texts: biblical, historical and musical. Most of our sources, the Levitical codes, revolutionary leaflets, spirituals, were produced, transmitted and received communally. A group/community consciousness represents the reality of most people on earth today and the great majority of people throughout history.

The work of the Jubilee Action Group is collective at many levels. The play comes out of a community-based popular theatre model. Production of the play involved collective writing, editing and stage directing. In terms of performance we are always working together and the play has no "stars." At the audience level we try to bring the play to existing groups alrady working on a particular issue or issues that connect to our reading of Jubilee.

Collective work also gives us particular insight for reading Jubilee. Jubilee and Sabbath economics are concerned with the common good; our identification with the Action Group and other groups we are part of—workers, students, poor—has helped us to see Jubilee as relevant beyond our individual situations. Many of us are involved in text-based action at a street level. We bring our "Jubilee Women

---

[56] Roland Murphy.

Against Poverty" banner to demonstrations. In the impoverished downtown core we covered walls and lampposts with *Jubilee is Coming!* stickers. In the financial district, we plastered banks with posters demanding "redistribute wealth" "cancel debts" and on expensive garment retailers "liberate slaves." We also support one another in various action campaigns—vigiling for affordable housing, protesting evictions, organizing with other women against globalization, marching against poverty and standing on picket lines.

To act for a cause, whether that action be to speak publicly, to leaflet at a demonstration or to risk arrest, increases one's commitment. We have learned from our experience in the Catholic Worker, the radical discipleship movement[57] and shorter-lived affinity groups, that to take visible political action based on a text, is to know that text in a profoundly different way than is possible through intensive exegesis, traditional liturgy or apolitical embodiment. Slaves who sang of the coming "Jubilee" and struggled for freedom, True Levellers who plowed the commons and Chartists who marched out on their Grand National Holiday, all had a sense of Jubilee. They were already enacting a program and enacting it with companions. In some sense these Jubilee scriptures are parallel texts of collective action. Women and men together put their bodies on the line, on the commons and on the streets because they believed Jubilee was relevant for the present rather than some impossible utopian dream which was never enacted in history.

To summarize, our developing hermeneutic of class, body and collective engagement/action operate at several levels. First of all this threefold hermeneutic is particularly effective for reading Jubilee texts. More generally, it is an approach to texts which is oriented toward their collective nature and socially transformative power, a way of reading the Bible which is often neglected in European and domi-

---

[57] Wes Howard Brook, "Reading For/About Our Lives: Politics, Poetics and Personhood in the Fourth Gospel." Presented to the Meeting of the Johannine Literature Section of the Society of Biblical Literature Annual Meeting in New Orleans, 25 November, 1996, 6.

nant church traditions. Beyond the Bible our hermeneutic provides avenues for moving easily between texts, biblical texts, historical texts and the texts of bodies. It thereby allows us to intersect with our audience and enables points of connection with their experience, regardless of the faith tradition from which they come.

Intersecting the Audience

Jubilaction is constantly evolving as we adapt the play to specific audiences and as audiences give us feedback on what has inspired them or changes they'd like to see. We have experimented with different formats at the end of the play—ranging from a two hour workshop to a ten minute discussion period. We have recently dropped the workshop because it seems to dilute the emotional power of the play, and we focus on discussion.

Music is central to the show, serving an almost liturgical function. We put songsheets on the chairs and we ask the audience to sing along at key transition moments between scenes. Here we tap into three traditions that have used music to liberate the spirit from the psychological bonds of oppression or to generate hope—African American spirituals, the music of the early trade union movement in Britain and North America, and the anglo folk music tradition of the 60's and 70's.

We have performed the play for a few church audiences, but have also encountered resistance there. Audience reactions are linked to class and race identity. In some middle-class church venues where only the tribal Israel scene has been performed responses have ranged from an expression of hopefulness to fear to "this is communism" and "what will it mean for me?"[58]

Among working class audiences, which have included Canadians from different races and ethnicities, members have been able to identify with the characters and stories. In the after-play discussion

---

[58] In their faith resource on Jubilee in 1998, Ten Days For Global Justice, a Canadian ecumenical church coalition, included the first scene of our play as a commentary on Leviticus. The scene has been acted out in many churches and youth groups in the Ten Days network across the country.

both anti-poverty and union audiences expressed excitement to discover part of their history, especially women's history. Several welfare
rights activists told us how good they felt to be part of such a history
of fighting injustice. After a performance at a union summer school
sixty women asked for copies of the script and the summer school
named its daily newsletter "Jubilee." A First Nations woman suggested we include the history of Indian slavery in Canada and
brought us a source book.[59]

These experiences taught us how the audience is also a partici-
pant in the play. The life situations of the audience and hence their
responses will always vary, and will contribute to the construction of
the meaning.[60] This is because we are not just conveying information
about events to the audience. We are telling a story.

> The story itself has energy and power. The story affects the
> whole person—heart, soul, mind and body... . Words and sto-
> ries are "speech acts." Something happens to the audience as a
> result of experiencing the story.[61]

Jubilaction has transformative power for pluralistic audiences because
it taps into a radical psychosocial function of theatre—recovering
historical memory—a historical memory of women's resistance and
of a radical vision of social change. The psychosocial and healing
function of recovering historical memory has been analysed by Jesuit
Ignacio Martin-Baro, the psychologist of liberation.[62] Martin-Baro
argued that one of the most urgent tasks facing political/liberation
psychology was recovering the historical memory of the peasant and
working classes in El Salvador in order to challenge the people's
sense of fatalism—that there is nothing they can do about oppressive

---

[59] Margarite D'Youville, foundress of the Grey Nuns, had at one time 236 Indian
slaves in her employment. Adams, *op. cit.* 55.

[60] Rhoads, op. cit. 107.

[61] Ibid. 108.

[62] Martin-Baro was one of the eight people murdered by the School of the Americas graduates in San Salvador at the University of Central America in 1989.

social conditions.[63] Jubilaction recovers the memory of resistance and a vision of justice that counteracts the fatalism many poor Canadians feel today.

Theatre can be either illustrative or transformative. *Jubilaction* functions as the latter, generating a sense of possibility, moving beyond fatalism, giving people a sense that they can fight injustice. This is because the play provides an aesthetic space, which has a capacity to be generative.[64] Audience members can imagine resistance in their own contexts.

In recovering the historical memory of working class women who were an active part of Jubilee, we restore Jubilee as both a working class and feminist memory. Not only does the audience discover that there is a biblically based radical tradition of struggling for justice and freedom for the poor, by the poor, but that women were part of these struggles, and often led them. For women and men who have been fighting poverty and oppression, the play affirms a sense of identity and pride in belonging to a tradition and a culture of resistance and liberation.

Conclusion: Teaching to Transgress [65]

Jubilaction as feminist popular theatre, provides a space for transgressing boundaries, of pointing to transformative possibilities. This is theatre both as pedagogy and as aesthetic space. The confluence of the methodology of feminist popular theatre with our cross-textual hermeneutic of class, bodies and collective engagement/action allow us to open up the particularistic religious tradition of Jubilee to a pluralistic audience. Jubilee reclaimed as an historical memory becomes a living tradition that inspires those audience members committed to a just world and the common good.

---

[63] Ignacio Martin-Baro, "Toward a Liberation Psychology," in *Writings for a Liberation Psychology*, eds. Adrianne Aron and Shawn Corne, (Boston: Harvard University Press, 1994), 30.

[64] Julie Salverson, *Performing Testimony: Ethics, Aesthecis and a Foolish Pedagogy*, unfinished PhD dissertation, U of T.

[65] bell hooks, *Teaching to Transgress: Education as the Practice of Freedom*, (New York: Routledge, 1994).

It is clear when we speak of a pluralistic audience that we have chosen "a way of speaking that is informed by the particularity and uniqueness of whom we are speaking to and with." [66] Our language speaks to working class people and to those who have made alliances with the poor and working class, of whatever faith background. In engaging the audience in the stories and the songs of Jubilee resistance we have neither privatized Jubilee nor have we claimed it has universal validity. Rather we have created moments of identification—as bodies, as exploited workers and the poor, and as actors in community—that bring the sacred texts alive in the present.

Archie C. C. Lee argues that the guiding principle in cross-textual hermeneutics is "the common human religious quest... the search for the encounter with the sacred in the mundane."[67] We have not given primacy to the Jubilee biblical texts; rather we see the sacred texts of women's lives, their interpretations and the living out of the Jubilee vision in different historical periods, as equally valid. This is because these texts "independently pose the same religious quest and address the similar religious dimensions of life,"[68] while deepening our understanding of the original text. The religious quest with which audience members identify is the search for the sacred in the struggle for liberation from injustice and oppression. Here the points of connection—collective action, suffering and healing bodies, and class identification—are reinscribed through the experience of feminist popular theatre

As theatre, as an exercise in cross-textual hermeneutics, *Jubilaction* promotes a transgression of culture—the dominant culture of unbridled accumulation—with the vision of radical equality and redistribution of wealth. It is in this "teaching to transgress" that *Jubilaction* speaks to a pluralistic yet specific audience out of the particularity of a tradition. Jubilee, a proletarian Jubilee, has meaning for

---

[66] Ibid. 11.

[67] Archie Lee, op.cit., 45.

[68] Ibid. 46.

working class people and their allies regardless of religious affiliation. In the uncovering and reclaiming of the subjugated knowledge of Jubilee resistance audiences recognize their own capacity for agency in the present.

Denise Nadeau is a feminist liberation theologian, dance therapist and popular educator living in British Columbia. She is currently working on her D. Min in International Feminism out of San Francisco Theological Seminary. Her e-mail address is dnadeau@web.net

Laurel Dykstra is an activist and worker-scholar in the Catholic Worker tradition. Her field is Hebrew Bible and her current project is a book exploring how first world readers can find ourselves in Exodus if we read from the perspective of the Egyptians. Laurel can be contacted at loraldyk@hotmail.com

Bibliography

Adams, Howard. *A Tortured People: The Politics of Colonization.* Penticton, BC: Theytus Books, 1995.

Balasuriya, Tissa. "Theological Reflections on the Way to Jubilee." Call to Action Conference, Detroit Michigan, November, 1998 (cassette).

Benbow, William. *Grand National Holiday and Congress of the Productive Classes.* ed. SEA. Bushnell. London: Pelagian Press, 1839.

Brevard, Lisa Pertillar. "'Will the Circle Be Unbroken:' African-American Women's Spirituality in Sacred Song Traditions." In *My Soul Is a Witness.* Gloria Wade-Gayles ed. Boston: Beacon Press, 1995: 32-47.

Casaldaliga, Don Pedro. "El Cuerno Del Jubileo: Jubileo 2000." Circular fraterna. January 1998. In *Jubileo Ano 2000*.CRIE. Mexico, July. 1998.

Centre for Social Justice. *The Growing Gap.* Toronto: Centre for Social Justice, 1998.

Davies, Stevie. *Unbridled Spirits: Women of the English Revolution, 1640-1660*. London: The Women's Press, 1998.

Epstein, Rachel. Editorial to *Participatory Research Newsletter, Special Issue on Popular Theatre*. Toronto, Spring 1987.

Federici, Sylvia. "Reproduction and Feminist Struggle in the New International Division of Labour." In Dalla Costa, Maria Rosa and G. Dalla Costa, eds. *Women, Development and the Labour of Reproduction: Issues of Struggles and Movements*. Lawrenceville, NJ: Africa World Press, 1998.

Frankel, Elen. *The Five Books of Miriam, A Woman's Commentary on the Torah*. San Francisco: HarperSanFrancisco, 1998.

Hill, Christopher. *The World Turned Upside Down*. London: Penguin, 1972.

hooks, bell. *Teaching to Transgress: Education as the Practice of Freedom*. New York: Routledge, 1994.

Howard Brook, Wes. "Reading For/About Our Lives: Politics, Poetics and Personhood in the Fourth Gospel." Presented to the Meeting of the Johannine Literature Section of the Society of Biblical Literature, Annual Meeting in New Orleans, 25 November, 1996.

Kwok Pui-lan and Elisabeth Schussler Fiorenza, eds. *Women's Sacred Scriptures*. Concilium. Maryknoll: Orbis Books, 1998.

Lee, Archie C. C. "Cross Textual Hermeneutics on Gospel and Culture." *Asian Journal of Theology* 10/1 1996, 38-48.

Linebaugh, Peter. "Jubilation: Or, How the Atlantic Working Class Used the Biblical Jubilee against Capitalism, With Some Success." In *The New Enclosures*, Midnight Notes Collective. New York: Automedia, 1990, 84-97.

Martin-Baro, Ignacio. "Toward a Liberation Psychology." In *Writings for a Liberation Psychology,* eds. Adrianne Aron and Shawn Corne, Boston: Harvard University Press, 1994.

Myers, Ched. "God Speed the Year of Jubilee! The Biblical Vision of Sabbath Economics." *Sojourners* 27/3,4 1998, 24-39, 36-39.

The Pan African Healing Foundation. "Conference Document" London: The Pan African Healing Foundation, September 8, 1998.

Ralte, Lalrinawmi, Florence Robinson, et al. eds. *Envisioning A New Heaven and A New Earth.* Delhi: NCCI/ISPCK, 1998.

Rue, Victoria. "'Cancerbodies:' *Women Speaking the Unspeakable. Feminist Theatre Enacts Feminist Theology.*" Unpublished Doctoral Thesis, Graduate Theological Union, 1994.

Salverson, Julie. "*Performing Testimony: Ethics, Aesthecis and a Foolish Pedagogy.*" Unfinished Ph.D dissertation, University of Toronto.

Schwarzkopf, Jutta. *Women in the Chartist Movement.* London: Macmillan, 1991.

Soelle, Dorothee. *Creative Disobedience.* Cleveland: The Pilgrim Press, 1995.

Thompson, Dorothy. *The Early Chartists.* London: Macmillan, 1971.

_____. *Outsiders: Class, Gender and Nation.* London: Verso Press, 1993.

Uko, Hans. ed. *The Jubilee Challenge: Utopia or Possibility?* Geneva: WCC Publications, 1997.

Walker, Margaret. *Jubilee.* New York: Bantam, 1966.

Waskow, Arthur. "Beyond Marx and Buddha: The Jubilee." In *God-wrestling,* New York: Schocken Books, 1978. 110-127

_____. "Holy Economics: A Rhythm of Worthy Work and Reflective Rest" *Sojourners* 26 (5 – 1997) 34-36.

11

Jubilee at the Turn of the 21st Century and the African Woman

Puleng Lenka-Bula

Introduction

> Jubilee is a time when those who have fallen on bad times have their freedom and property restored. Jubilee, the year of the restoration, serves a dual purpose. It reminds the people that land belongs to God; and it prevents the wealthy from amassing land.[1]

We, African Women theologians, ethicists and activists, who are committed to the pursuit for justice and abundant life for all creation of God, and for all humanity cannot begin to reaffirm our understanding of Jubilee at the turn of the century until we acknowledge and address the death-dealing and life negating realities such as poverty, gender injustices and inequality, the impact and effects of debt, globalisation and the liberalisation of the African economies on African women, children and men.

I strongly believe that Jubilee should move beyond the campaign for the cancellation of debt, the redistribution and restoration of land, the provision of freedom to those enslaved by economic injustices. Jubilee as well, should be broadened to embrace the articulation for justice for African women, men and children who are affected by the HIV/AIDS epidemic which affects drastically almost all African communities. AIDS in Southern Africa is exacerbated by the inaccessibility of AIDS medication which have high potential to reduce the levels of infection. Multinational and Transnational pharmaceutical companies are hoarding and refusing to sell HIV drugs such as AZT at a nominal and affordable price. The hoarding of patents and trademarks by these pharmaceutical companies exhibit the ideal that profit is important to humanity. This ethos should be redressed.

---

[1] Alexander, P. and M. [eds], *The Lion Handbook to the Bible*, 1986, 181.

This paper aims at locating the imperative for Jubilee at the turn of this century for African women. The analysis of poverty, debt, gender inequality and injustice and the effects of globalisation and liberalisation of the African economies on African communities, women, men, children will enable us to understand why Jubilee is not just a campaign for freedom, redistribution and restoration of land, debt and bondage to those oppressed by those who are economically powerful but it is the campaign for the restoration of meaningful Life for all.

Jubilee for an African womanist theologian and ethicist like me, refers to the articulation of life. It refers to the call, the cry and the invitation to those who are in positions of economic power to say, "please let me live the life that God granted me in full. It means, please do not render my life in this world redundant by limiting my existence and growth."

The basic faith questions undergirding this paper include: What does Jubilee mean for African and Basotho women in particular in the 21st century? In the event of the perpetual cultural, patriarchal and gender injustices and inequalities does Jubilee have anything to say to women? In the context of globalisation and rampant increase of HIV/AIDS in Africa does the campaign for jubilee address the needs of women and children living with HIV/AIDS? One is also bound to ask the question, How does the cancellation of debt by the major financial institutions and Northern governments translate to the lives of the marginalized and poverty-stricken African women, men and children?

The next section of this paper will discuss the relationship of poverty, debt, globalisation and liberalisation of the African economies and gender inequalities. The exploration of these issues will highlight the relevance for the campaign for Jubilee 2000. I shall in this paper use as my methodology, a hermeneutical circle of praxis which is open-ended. Womanists, feminists and liberation theologians and ethicists often utilise this process. The basic belief underlying this methodology is that the lives and concrete situations of people must shape theology.

Poverty is explained and defined in diverse ways depending on the location of whoever is providing a poverty definition. Unlike statisticians, demographers and some economists who prefer to use statistics and numerical presentations of poverty, I believe that the lived experiences of poverty, provide and highlight better the effects of poverty in southern Africa. The stories and experiences of poverty enable us to understand the imperative for the articulation of justice and a call for Jubilee. These experiences provide clues to issues of justice, of responsibilities and the pursuit for life. Their analysis provide the basis for the search for alternatives against poverty. Karen Lebacqz suggests that reflections on justice should begin with the "realities of Injustice."[2]

> If justice begins with the correction of injustices, then the most important tools for understanding justice will be the stories of injustice as experienced by the oppressed, and the tools of social and historical analysis that help to illumine the process by which those historical injustices arose and their meaning in the lives of the victims.[3]

The realities of poverty depicted in this paper cover the experiences of Black African Women and men in the context of Lesotho and South Africa where I have been raised and have lived for the most part of my life.

Poverty: The Basis for the Invitation and Cry for Jubilee

I also attempt through story-telling to establish the context of women's experiences of poverty in South Africa. This context forms and informs the reflection of poverty and its impact on the poor. The implications of poverty on the poor challenge us and our churches to respond practically to these situations.

Faces of Poverty

Story-telling is important in that it takes seriously the notion affirmed above, that our experiences inform and form the questions we ask about life and death. In addition, story telling affirms the womanist and feminist notion that, "the personal is political," hence the critical interrelationship between the individual experience to the collective.

---

[2] Karen Lebacqz,. *Justice in an Unjust World: Foundations for a Christian Approach to Justice.* 1987, 10

[3] Karen Lebaqz,. "Implications for a Theology of Justice," In Boulton, W. et al [eds] *From Christ to the World: Introductory Readings,* 1994, 254.

I intend in the next section to relate stories of women reflecting their experiences of poverty in South Africa. The first story relates to women working in the industrial sector, told in the *Women's National Coalition News* of October 1993. While this story was written in 1993, it still reflects the mentality of many factories and industries in many third world countries where 'sweat-shops' have become the order of the day and remain unchallenged.

Women's Experiences

> Four hundred women in Natal Midlands have left their jobs demanding what other women all over the world take for granted: the right to wear their panties at work. According to company rules, they have to wash and take off their panties on arrival at work and replace with company issued Bermuda shorts. The company says new chicks easily catch diseases and there need to be strict hygiene measures.[4] A male supervisor touches our private parts to ensure that we are not wearing panties. Some of us are married and our husbands find this insulting and some have asked their wives to stop working.[5] Imagine having to tell your children that you can't work with your panties on.[6]

The second story relates the experience of a woman drawn from an interview I had with a friend whose cousin lives in abject poverty:

> Alina is a single woman recently widowed. She has three children aged 19, 10 and 3. She has recently been retrenched from work in a printing and publishing company in which she worked for 11 years. She had worked in this company as an office assistant, and occasionally helped with typing, filing and binding books. Alina is currently unemployed. She has sought other jobs and has not been able to find a job. She has consequently decided to start a small business. Her target will be poor people who cannot afford to buy food providing people with protein as cheese; eggs and meat are relatively expensive. She intends to sell chicken feet,

---

[4] Women's National Coalition News. October 1993, 2

[5] Ibid. 2

[6] Ibid. 2

head and offal to these communities. The money generated from this business will be used to support the family and to help in the children's education.[7]

The third story is drawn from the poverty hearings of the South African NGO Coalition. It is a story of Julia Kotelo who lives in Mpumalanga. She says,

> In the past we were settled at Loskop dam. My grandfather lived there. We had a homestead. We were removed to other places. First to Parys. We were removed again to where we are now. My grandfather had many cattle, sheep goats. Now we are on a small place. The herd has no grazing place. They have died. Nothing is left now. My father failed to educate us because he was looking after the cattle. Our children will also not go to school. When we were moved to Loskop, a white man occupied the land. He was farming it for his children. When he got rich he sold the land to the government. Now it is a game lodge. It has brought poverty to us. Loskop has water but not us. It is only 10 kilometres away, but the water passes us. The water is made for whites only. We want access to it for irrigation and to look after our children.

The fourth stories relates to the story of Basotho Agricultural migrant workers.

> A group of Basotho women queue at the Ministry of Agriculture to be listed as prospective migrant workers to the farms in South Africa. The ministry recruits women and men, young and healthy to work in the agricultural industry of South Africa. These women leave Lesotho at the end of August and come back to Lesotho on the 22nd of December for a 10 days leave from their work. They return to South Africa in January and finish their contracts in March. These women and men are not allowed to go to their places of work with children as this exacerbates the statistics of the so-called "Alien Immigrants" in South Africa.

The fifth story relates to the problems encountered by squatter campers in Sandton, Johannesburg:

---

[7] This paper is told in Poverty and Education in South Africa, 1998, 31

Sandton is an affluent suburb in the northern parts of Johannesburg. It is characterized by big mansions, several shopping malls and expensive prices of land. Sandton is regarded as an up-market commercial area of Gauteng Province. In 1996, groups of Black people set up their houses adjacent to Sandton. These people received a lot of animosity as the residents of Sandton campaigned for their evictions. The owners of property in Sandton, alleged that squatter camps in their locality were reducing and degrading the value of their property. The poverty stricken people living in squatter camps argued that they needed a place to put up their shelter, and the space they had settled in, was not occupied by anyone. The affluent community of Sandton, put up a fence and a gate that controlled the influx of who was permitted to enter the area and who was to be disallowed to enter this area. This controversy was covered by some newspapers such as *Sowetan*. Finally, squatter campers who were just advocating for the right to shelter were evicted from Sandton by the Alexander municipality.

HIV /AIDS and Poverty and South Africa

HIV/AIDS activists, people living with HIV/AIDS and the Gay and Lesbian Coalition of South Africa gathered around the American Embassy in Acadia Pretoria. Poor people who are infected by AIDS find the medication expensive and inaccessible. Big pharmaceutical companies refuse to reduce the prices of the drugs which can reduce the levels and or the weakening of the body system. For these people, medication without proper nursing care, without the political will by transnational companies, mean the perpetuation of their condition.

The stories of women in particular and of the southern African communities illustrated above depict typical experiences of many women in South Africa who live with poverty. These examples however do not see the experiences of all South African women as homogenous. There are other women who live in situations of affluence, and they do not form the focus of this study. I shall in the next section engage in an analysis of poverty.

Socio-Economic and Political Analysis of Poverty

The stories of women told above reflect the fact that poverty is multi-dimensional and constitutes a network of interrelated deprivations, which reinforce each other.[8] The first story of the women working in the poultry industry reveal the dehumanizing conditions that poverty leads women into. It also displays the profit maximization imperative, which is core to the principles and values of the capitalist market economy. The company rule that women should remove their underwear at work kills their integrity and their humanity. It is obvious that the company is only interested in generating profit and has no interest in maintaining human rights at work.

One is bound to ask questions such as, why would women agree to work under humiliating conditions such as these? What did these women do to counter this requirement? Did they just become passive and helpless and continue to do their jobs as the employers required? According the Women's Coalition Newsletter, Women workers at NCF picketed outside supermarkets in Longmarket Street persuading shoppers to boycott NCF products."[9]

There are lessons to be learned from this experience. The women did not become complacent to the rule that denied them their right to be fully human. They mobilised and engaged the broader society to be aware of the conditions they worked under. Moreover, these women educated their communities about the atrocities that women face in the place of work, thus conscientizing the communities about the ethic underlying the products they consume. This is one step in ensuring that the corporate sector becomes socially and ethically responsible.

The story of Alina's retrenchment is symbolic of the current phenomena of retrenchments, downsizing and cutbacks that the corporate and public sector is presently fervently embarking on. The third story of Julia Kotelo reveals the relationship of poverty with the global market economy that destroys local subsistence economy to dependence and subjugation to poverty. The land that provides food for people and animals, which provides homes for the people and on which the

---

[8] S. Vally et al., "Poverty and Education in South Africa," 1998, 4
[9] *Women's Coalition Newsletter.* 1993: 2

survival of the people depends is sold and turned into a holiday resort for entertainment. The story of Basotho women Agricultural migrant workers and of the people who had set up their "Tin" houses in Sandton exhibits Communal poverty. According to Peter Donaldson, community poverty "manifests itself where almost everyone in a community is poor."[10] In South Africa and Lesotho there are several situations that depict the situation of community poverty. For Example, in Maseru, men who usually come to the city to find jobs and end up in the streets in Maseru due to unemployment and lack of jobs are often referred to in a derogatory name that they are "Bo Mpokho." This name is given to them because they sleep in the mountain under the caves in a mountain called Mpokho.

The story of the woman working as a domestic worker for a white woman in Wynburg, explains the experience of poverty which Donaldson refers to as, "Case poverty." This poverty is experienced in both affluent and poverty-stricken communities. The visibility of the suffering of an individual is so conspicuous when compared to the living conditions of people around them. For example, Kate Ntombekazi's experience of living in the streets, exposes her to a situation of vulnerability where she works for an income and her increase in salary is dependent on her age and not the amount of work she does for her employer. Do these experiences have any significance for the call for justice, Jubilee and cancellation of debt for our countries, our people and our communities?

Poverty and Gender Injustice

There are multiple issues which create the conditions and situations of poverty for African Women. These include, gender injustices manifested through the oppression of women and denying them a meaningful place in charting the direction of economic, political and socio-cultural decisions in Lesotho and in South Africa. Currently, South Africa boasts that it has the most progressive constitution in Africa, which engenders the rights of women and which values gender equality.

---

[10] P. Donaldson, *Worlds Apart: The Economic Gulf Between Nations*, 2

Many South Africans argue that the establishment of the Gender Commission headed by Ms Joyce Seroke signifies the huge strides made in ensuring women's rights. The unfortunate thing is that, whilst the constitution is so protective of women, and while women Parliamentarians in South Africa make up a relatively high number when compared to other African Countries, the reality is that at a practical level, women are abused, sexually harassed and exploited the most. According to the People Against Women Abuse, [an organisation in South Africa] a woman is raped every three minutes in South Africa. Does this have any link to women living in poverty? Do these women expose themselves to this sexual violence? I doubt it. Many poor women like Kate, who work as domestic workers, are subjected to abuse, exploitation and no legal protection against those who exploit them. This is similar to the experience of women who migrate to South African to work in the farms.

Linking Poverty to Gender Injustices and Globalisation

Globalisation in too many instances creates, maintains and promotes the inequalities between men and women, between poorer and affluent nations and between those who are affluent and those who live in poverty. Because globalisation is based in the market and competitive imperative, those who are unable to compete with the giants are swallowed up and or made redundant. The immoral ethos of "survival of the fittest" translated in the economic policies of our national countries, such as Structural Adjustment Programmes in Lesotho and Growth and Employment and Redistribution Programme in South Africa, consequently degrade life for those who are poor.

Poverty and Globalisation

Poverty can be linked to the current market economy, which finds expression in globalisation. The description of globalisation by "Economic Justice in South Africa: A Pastoral Letter," by the Catholic Church in South Africa is important for our understanding of the relationship of poverty, globalisation and the link with the feminisation of poverty. This pastoral letter explains globalisation in the following words:

With each passing year, methods of communication and transport become faster and more sophisticated. Decisions made in one country are implemented almost immediately on the other side of the world. Multinational companies operate in numerous countries around the world, and many of them are vastly more powerful, from an economic point of view, than many developing nations. Trade controls and restrictions on the flow of money from one country to another are constantly being eliminated. Taken together, these changes in the international economic order are known as globalisation.[11]

In some ways, globalisation has some positive elements such as the promotion of speedy communication, transport and other things. However, its negative impact on African in general and women in particular surpass the positive attributes it yields. The Catholic Bishop's Conference points out that the negative impact of globalisation functions in ways which "threaten the well-being and development of the poorer nations."[12]

The experiences reflected above can be linked to the current globalized market economy, which South Africa has adopted through its formulation and implementation of the macro-economic policy of Growth, Employment and Redistribution commonly known as GEAR. This policy has radically shifted from the Reconstruction and Development programme, which it adopted as its policy after the 1994 democratic election.

In 1994, the government made a commitment that central to the government plan, was a "commitment to effectively address the problem of poverty and the gross inequality evident in almost all aspects of South African Society."[13] This commitment was unfortunately eroded in 1996 when government shifted its policy to "voluntary Structural Adjustment policies which primarily focus on international competitiveness and economic growth."[14] The main feature of GEAR can be

---

[11] Southern African Catholic Bishops Conference. "Economic Justice in South Africa: A Pastoral Statement," 1999, 28.

[12] Ibid., 28

[13] RDP White Paper 1994: i.

[14] S. Vally et al., *Poverty and Education in South Africa*, 1998, 5.

summarised as, aggressive liberalisation of trade which results in the creation of free trade, privatisation, reduction of state expenditure, down-sizing and reduction of civil service staff, export-oriented economy, wage restraint, a flexible labour market which can be easily hired and fired, and generous tax concessions for the corporate sector.

It is important to note that the economic policies encouraged and implemented by the government further entrench the poverty of women. This phenomenon is known as the feminization of poverty. The emphasis on economic growth by the government marginalises the quests and attempts by women for socio-economic justice. This entrenches further pauperization of the women.

Carmelita Usog, an Asian theologian, suggests that poverty is not only the result of economic policies which value profit more than other things, it is also entrenched by kyriarchy.[15] She says, the evil of kyriarchy let loose in the Third World or the South breeds poverty, violence and degradation and exploitation and the hardest hit are women. She reflects on the poem written by a Roman Catholic Nun, Maria L. David that portrays the lives of the women living in poverty. The fist two stanzas of this poem read as follows:

I have been stripped of my basic necessities
my stomach craved for food to appease
the pangs of hunger
my back longed for a decent bed
or even bamboo slats
to ease out my tired muscles from the days labour
Cries of starving children chorused
prompting me to listen
shouts of humiliation were the lot of mothers
who continued the shout of food.
Misery, poverty become an institution
made heavier and stronger by wealth and power
starved individuals.

---

[15] Kyriarchy is a technical term which refers to the relationship of a master over a servant. This is a hierarchical relationship is based on abuse of power, manipulation and exploitation.

sapping every minute possession of
the poor and exploited ones.

This poem reflects on the experiences of women as well as it embraces the critic of greed. The contents of this poem also embrace and relate to the stories of poverty which depict the context of poverty in South Africa. What are the alternatives to these situations? Can the Church play a liberative role in the lives of those who are poverty-stricken? I am convinced that it is our duty and responsibility to work with those who are poor. The message and work of the church therefore should to exhibit a preferential option for the poor as the Latin American theologian Gustavo Guttierez suggests.

Are There Any Alternatives?

The church is required to respond to poverty. The role that theology can play in the context of poverty is very profound in the midst of these glaring situations. Mercy Amba Oduyoye and Carol Robb encourage us Christians to proclaim the liberative message of hope which characterized Jesus' message, community and work amongst and within his society. They also claim that the liberative hope can be drawn from the Bible. They caution us that, despite the tendency of the Bible to contain patriarchal and oppressive stories, it also proclaims the liberative and hopeful message for the people of God. This emancipatory message must opt for the oppressed and the poor. Robb says, Justice is the main principle for evaluating life, for evaluating economy and law. Above all, justice is also the personality of God. These theologians invite and challenge us to participate in the efforts that aim at breaking the chains and cycles of poverty.

Attempts to alleviate poverty also exemplify the notion of justice as pragmatic, practical, achievable, historical and necessary. Dr. Molefe Tsele, also suggests that justice becomes obstructed when the church does not articulate Biblical justice in the articulation of life through its theological and ethical reflection. This means our churches should avoid status quo theologies which reduces the poor to passivity and promises them comfort in the next life.

We can therefore draw our hope and participate in seeking justice from biblical texts such as, the story of The Bent Over Woman in the Gospel of Luke. Also important is the practice of Jubilee, in which the poor were forgiven their debts and given back their property after a period of seven years. In contemporary life, this Jubilee can be achieved by establishing programmes, funds, trust and community strategies which help the poor. A better structured welfare system could enable the poor of South Africa to engage in activities, which will enable the poor to live their life fully. The churches can participate by being morally creative and accountable to those they minister to. For Marilyn, Legge, this responsibility is translated through acts of solidarity with the poor and with those in situations of suffering. She suggests that solidarity be understood as a contemporary expression for grace aimed at living out and proclaiming justice as the good news. Solidarity, in my view, refers to the active participation in making real the vision of abundant life for all humanity and the cosmos.

The church can also participate in the campaign for Jubilee 2000. This campaign calls for the cancellation of the debts of the poorest countries by multi-lateral governments and financial institution such as the World Bank and the International Monetary Fund, as this debt relegates many to situations of poverty and helplessness.

Conclusion

Our efforts will not make sense or will not be sufficient if we maintain distance from those who are affected by poverty. Exploring poverty as academic exercises as it is displayed by many poverty studies commissioned by the ecumenical movement in South Africa coupled with no practical attempts to alleviating the result of such studies, dis-empowers the poor. I believe that our efforts at empowering each other should derive also from our African theology of life and the notion of "Botho' of humaness and being human with each other. We should alleviate poverty and continue in affirming life as our sisters and brothers at the seminar on "Sustaining Life in the Context of Globalisation" stated: "We love life and want this life to be lived by our people with dignity."[16] The effects of poverty on women are complex. They vary and depend on the diverse situations of women in the home, communities and their countries. Poverty for women is also influenced by external factors such as the economic relationship of our country to the major financial institutions such as the World Bank, the International Monetary fund and other financial sources such as governments of the affluent northern countries like the United States of America, Britain and other European and North American countries. Women's situations of poverty are also influenced by culture, religions and development structures, policies and strategies which reinforce patriarchal and kyriarchal control. The basic problem experienced by people living in and with poverty is that they are denied the right to life. They suffer from malnutrition, alienation and dehumanisation. Like the people living in "Tin" houses in Alexander who are evicted from their homes, these men who do not have shelter who are referred to in derogatory words, are deprived of the dignity and integrity of being human. They are alienated from the society and are made to feel unwanted and redundant. Poverty therefore deprives people their integrity and their humanity.

Paper presented to the Circle of Concerned African Women Theologians 10th Anniversary—Accra, Ghana, 5-10 October 1999.

Puleng Lenka-Bula is a theologian from Lesotho currently working as a researcher for the Institute for Contextual Theology, South Africa

---

[16] Abraham, K. C. et. al *Voices From the Third World* . 1998: 134

Bibliography

Abraham, K. C. [ed] *Voices From the Third World: Theology in The Context of Globalisation.* Vol. XXI/1 Evanston: American Theological Library Association, 1998.

Abraham, K. C. *Voices From the Third World: Women Reflecting On Gender, Power, and Theology.* Vol. XXI/2. Evanston: American Theological Library Association, 1998

Case. *Poverty and Religion.* Johannesburg: Community Agency for Social Enquiry, 1998.

Lenka-Bula, Puleng. *"I am because we are." An African Womanist Theological and Ethical Reflection on Structural Adjustment Programmes of the World Bank and the International Monetary Fund.* [unpublished] Saskatoon: St Andrew's Theological College, 1997

Oduyoye, Mercy A. *Hearing and Knowing: Theological Reflections on Christianity in Africa.* New York: Orbis Books. 1986.

_____. *Reconstruction and Development Programme.* White Paper, 1994

Russell, L. M and Clarkson J.S. eds. *Dictionary of Feminist Theology.* Louisville: John Knox Westminister Press, 1996.

The Peoples Voices: National Speakout on Poverty Hearings. Johannesburg: SANGOCO, 1998.

Women's National Coalition News. Fourth Issue. Johannesburg: Women's National Coalition. 1993

Vally, Salim et al. *Poverty and Education in South Africa.* Poverty Hearings Background Paper. Johannesburg: Sangoco.

12

Towards a New Jubilee Covenant:
A Contribution from the Jubilee South

Jubilee South

Principles

Our starting point is Jubilee not debt. The announcement of Jubilee as an indictment of ALL unjust social and gender structures, the liberation of the entire web of human relationships and the restitution of the missing global community by moving forward in social justice.

Marginalised people everywhere—the oppressed of the Global South—demand and require a *political and solidarity* framework. That is, one based on recognition of the political primacy of those who suffer and struggle, of the survivors and those who resist—this means, the people of the South. Nothing about them without them. We should take our lead from them and from the movements and organisations they have spawned.

At stake is not simply the debt "issue" but the future of development aid itself highlighted by the cruel people-sacrificing advocacy of providing "support" only to "well run" countries.[1] As if people should be punished further for having bad governments; as if it has not been shown over and over again that the neoliberal "well run" seal of approval leads to impoverishment, no matter what the statistical manipulation.

Jubilee, if true to its core message, will contest Washington's determination to remake every other economy and culture in its own image. We need to denounce (not engage) these and any other pretexts to further abandon moral imperative and political responsibility of the rich governments and societies to redress the impoverishment in the South and have a closer look at the origins and environmental implications of obscene wealth concentration.

---

[1] World Bank, "Assessing Aid, What Works, What Doesn't, and Why," November, 1998, World Bank website: www.worldbank.org/research/aid

We feel it fundamental for Jubilee/debt campaigns to deal with the ecological debt of the North with the environment and the South. The recognition that the North has benefited from the natural and human resources of the South, and continues to do so by pushing a development model that entails the destruction of habitats, extinction, impoverishment and marginalisation of peoples, principally in the South.

Conditionality is a trap designed to sell civil societies, North and South, on the benefits of Northern-defined conditionality, both political and economic, at the expense of an already dwindling sovereignty and hence democratic self-determination. Let us not contribute to the further loss of control of policy-making—the issue is not simply economic, it is political and at stake is critical processes and paths of identity, including the right to be different.

It is time we recognise that creditors, including the G-7, cannot be trusted to redress the crisis that they created. The G-7 has not delivered. They failed to deliver on pledges in Cologne, just as they failed to deliver in Río, Copenhagen, Cairo and Beijing. Let us distinguish therefore between failed policies and failed politics. Because their policies will go unmodified unless we seriously review our politics, including the underlying power analysis.

G-7 failings as a whole make it imperative for campaigns in the North to focus on 100 percent unilateral cancellation by creditor governments to maximum number of poor countries.

This is not a question of relief but of justice: to put an end to the amply documented net transfers of wealth from the South to the North at the cost of intolerable suffering and sacrifices.

We need to recognise that the transfer of resources is effected both by debt and unfair trading practices. Proof enough is that the G-7's New Internationalism, proclaimed to be based on values and that justifies "humanitarian" intervention, does not carry over into the economic order.

The debt of the South has been amply "repaid." Nothing is owed! Cessation of debt payments is meaningful only in a framework of an end to structural adjustment programs and the introduction of taxation of financial transactions.

Jubilee campaigns everywhere should point out in no uncertain terms that debt "relief" that leaves structural adjustment conditions in force or reinforced is nothing less than unmitigated hypocrisy. No negotiation framework that countenances structural adjustment is morally engageable. Any mobilisation effort must have such assumptions explicitly at its core. Unless a mass movement is explicit in its demands and paradigm challenges, it can be subject of confusion and disillusion harmful to future education and hence sustained mobilisation for fuller changes in the global economy.

Cologne spelled the extension of Highly Indebted Poor Country Initiative and the reinforcement of the plundering power of the IMF. It was not a step forward or getting half way. There, the announced cancellations amounts to a maximum of US $25 billion, about 1 percent of the total world debt (US $2030 billion, excluding the Eastern bloc, according to the April World Bank report)—or no more than 12 percent of the 41 poorest countries' debt ($41 billion). Our mobilisation was successful in getting debt on the G-7 agenda; it was not successful in getting the G-7 to seriously tackle it.

At least G-7 governments recognised the need to respond to citizenry and to urgently address the debt question, however inadequately. In contrast most governments in the South have enjoyed an undeserved free ride. Our bureaucrats and technocrats are happy to have the Jubilee movements act as their professional lobbyists, at no cost to themselves. However, people's movements in the South know better than to plead on behalf of mostly incompetent and corrupt governments. Which is why an entirely different "debt repudiation" movement is gaining ground at the level of people that are putting not only their governments, but also NGOs and Churches in the North and South to the test.

It is up to us—the Jubilee movements—not the Bretton Woods institutions, not the G-7, not the governments of the South, to define the better deal for our people: the profound vision of justice embodied in the Jubilee ideal.

Shaping a New Mobilisation Strategy

Campaigns and movements need not be in contradiction. Campaign focuses on what are termed achievable goals tend to be focused and short-lived. But it is often forgotten that a campaign is one small piece of a larger picture of justice and structural change. Campaigns must contribute toward, and not detract from, movements.

The practice of human solidarity should not be conditioned on or by the generation of compassion, press campaigns or celebrity mobilisation.

Jubilee cannot afford to become subject to charity fatigues, episodic and superficial press management or fickle or trivialising media extravaganzas. Elite strategy and lobbying has its role, its limitations and above all its dangers: the danger of becoming morally implicated in the consequences of pseudo-reform.

Language is critical, and we are all challenged to review our own language in, along with our methods of, trying to achieve justice. Moral posturing is not acceptable. Jubilee South calls for the unapologetic and explicit defence of the primacy of the people's political over the corporate political that go under the guise of the technical. In terms of engagement, there is a need from both but the ethical and moral cannot be subordinated to the "viable" and the "pragmatic," let alone the technical and the macro-economic.

The thematic axis of a Jubilee campaign should link external debt with social debt and odious debt, as part of neoliberal adjustment policies. This means the linking of Debt Campaign and movements with the ATTAC Movement (Action for Taxing Transactions on behalf of Citizens) as connected and complementary campaigns.

Support for national and regional campaigns calling for public audits, debt tribunals and popular referendums as a strategic targets in the South; lobbying G-7 members may be a subsidiary target in South debt movements, but technical evidence and shame alone will not change policies.

It is not for campaigns in the South to be integrated into predefined campaigns in the North. If platforms are to be created they must respond primarily to the South. Campaigns in the North should dialogue extensively with counterparts in the North before assuming public positions in regard to so-called positive conditionality. Jubilee as a whole must be configured, politically and strategically, to deal with the integral challenges so as not to win partial concessions (on debt) at the expense of larger issues (trade and conditionality).

Credibility with the bankers and governments cannot come at the expense of credibility with the excluded. Working toward "sustainable debt" and "co-responsibility" are non-starters, historically and morally. Those who invented debt bondage will not be the ones to deliver us from it. It is high time for the G-7 and other rich countries to abandon the assumption that they know what is best for those they have impoverished.

We need a focused campaign that can relate to the integrity of struggle and consciousness, as people do not neatly divide their lives according to campaign "issues." This requires thinking of movements that spring campaigns and continue to grow, as opposed to temporary campaigns where we lose sight of the prophetic Jubilee call for structural transformation. We need to review not only debt, but also systems of finance, trade, production and consumption.

Different campaigns will and must respond to their domestic conditions, and must define their contributions accordingly. One thing is a respectful division of labour and complementing, *where complementarity* is possible.

Forget about "debt management" and "debt relief." Let governments and bankers work on that. For the North, Jubilee should begin or continue to focus on the cancellation *of morally uncollectable debt*—and not be afraid to address it as such.

As for the South, we should accelerate and support new and old movements *for outright unilateral debt repudiation* as demanded democratically by people. Where we can ally ourselves with governments let us do so, and where we cannot, let us stop following creditor and agency prescriptions for civil society and government covenants.

We must confront (not "dialogue") the new wave of G-7 WB/IMF arguments linking "relief" and even "aid" to the pursuit of "sound economic policies" and "good governance."[2] Flawed by se-

---

2 "...mainstream aid shoul be directed only to countries with sound economic management. The HIPC debt-relief plans, to their credit, do this. More donors

lective data and politically conditioned methodology, these studies reflect pre-existing biases, as though the social costs human misery can ever be reduced to numbers.

We call on Jubilee movements to mark their distance now from a "debt relief" and even "debt cancellation" framework where decisions are almost entirely made by creditor governments and client states.

Let us not again assume the risk of asking too little and then face the prospect, once again as in Cologne, of being demanded we congratulate the G-7. Let us learn to distinguish between those who say that they are on our side and those who say they are but really are not. We are accountable to the former, never to the latter. Let us say who we are.

A new Millennium gives birth to a New Hope—the hope for eradication of debt and indebtedness. We must not defraud that hope. We should be loyal to that mobilisation. This is the new paradigm.

A New Beginning for Jubilee 2000

We in the Jubilee movements unite out of sense of renewed possibilities. Our sense of hope is not a simple by-product of inspiration and faith. It is the product of analysis, of proximity to people's suffering but especially of the of the multiplication evidence of resistance North and South. We must reflect and consequently reinforce the increasing receptiveness to the critiques of corporate capitalism in all of its global and local manifestations.

Jubilee must pick up the pieces, gain new adherents and humbly seek the understanding of those whose commitment never had a time limit. The struggle for global economic and social justice has no time limit.

We in Jubilee South call on all forces and campaigns, North and South, not to give up. To continue to work with even greater determination and with the courage to discern between what can and cannot be sacrificed in our drive toward economic justice. We in the South demand that campaigners do what you constantly say you want

---

should follow suit." ("Helping the Third World," *The Economist*," June 26, 1999, 25).

to do. At the same time recognise, there can be no effective redressing of North/South relations or effective debt action if the people of the South are not directly involved. This is less a question of influencing governments than it is of following the poor.

If Jubilee is to become a global movement, it requires a vision and a program. A vision that comes from Jubilee and from the heritage of anti-colonial struggle, including anti-neo-colonial and to resistance today to neoliberal globalisation. This means total, unconditional and immediate cancellation of the debt.

Our challenge is to build bridges to build that global movement that will take us to the vision. We know that the times are not good for such movement-building, but that only makes it more necessary to build, and to build by educating and mobilising in stages of increasing complexity.

If we have been somewhat successful at mobilising we have been less successful at educating, particularly in the North, in generating consciousness of the links between debt and the other manifestation of economic oppression, and the resistance to those manifestations (Tobin Tax, ESAFs, capital liberalisation, MAI, WTO).[3] *This in part is because we have not made our moral/historical arguments with sufficient force.*

Hence the centrality of a shift toward a strong "illegitimate/immoral debt" strategy especially in the North accompanied, especially in the South, by a parallel push toward repudiation. Refusal to pay must be seen as the moral and logical outcome of something illegitimate or reprehensible. We in the South will continue to say that the debt has already been paid. We urge our counterparts in the North to insist that any payment is immoral because it could not be done without the imposition of ethically sanctionable hardship. A

---

[3] "If the G8 governments are genuinely concerned about poverty and impoverishment, they should accompany initiatives for debt cancellation with reforms of the financial and trading systems and also respond positively to the demand for greater control of the transnational flow of capital by governments and civil society. ... Their response has supported the Multilateral Agreement on Investments and increased power for the World Bank, IMF and WTO and, through them, for Transnational Corporations." (World Council of Churches, "Statement on the Debt Crisis," June 9, 1999).

repudiation strategy in the North is of a different nature, perhaps, than repudiation in the South. They complement each other although they are not the same.

> International solidarity is not an act of charity. It is an act of unity among allies fighting on different terrains toward the same objec tives. The foremost of these objectives is to aid the development of humanity to the highest level possible. — Samora Moisés Machel

Jubilee South is a growing and increasingly cohesive group of persons, coalitions and organisations that began to come together as groupings from the South within the worldwide Jubilee 2000 movement. Coming from all parts of the South they are united in their desire to strengthen and move beyond present Jubilee Debt campaigns through the presence and projection of a Jubilee South vision and voice.

13

Nurturing a Spirituality of Social Conversion

Michel Andraos

As Christians and people of faith in the God of life, we are called to make some urgent ethical choices. A social conversion towards the common good of all in our society—locally and globally, and towards harmony with mother earth and the environment is necessary. What is becoming clear to us as we understand better the root causes of social and ecological injustice at a global scale, is the violence embedded in our economic, political and cultural systems. These social systems of violence translate into interpersonal violence which we experience at many levels.

New voices from our churches and faith communities continue to reiterate the call for a radical social transformation; there are serious ethical problems at the root of our political and economic choices as a society which need to be addressed.[1] The problems are structural, at the heart of the systems, and what we need is a radically new social vision. We need to re-think our way of life and reverse the systems of social violence. This call for radical social transformation I name as *social conversion.*

The term "social conversion" as such is not frequently used in religious or theological language. In dictionaries of Christian social thought, the term does not exist as a developed concept, and it is not identified as a common experience or praxis. We find in the social Christian literature of the recent years frequent reference to "social evil" and "sinful structures," "but not to "social conversion." The term "conversion" is commonly used in Christian tradition to denote

---

[1] Just to name one example, I quote from the open address of the Moderator of the United Church of Canada from last spring: "Many Canadians are deeply disturbed by our market-driven economy, which changes people from citizens into consumers, distorts reality, demeans the human spirit, and plunders the earth. They know something is terribly wrong. Caught in the tentacles of principalities and powers beyond our control, we search for leadership, analysis and initiatives which respond to the depth and diversity of the human spirit." Bill Phipps, "An Invitation to Respond," Consultation about Faith and the Economy, United Church of Canada, 1999,<www.faith-and-the-economy.org>.

a radical personal transformation and change of direction in life; making a radically different choices as a result of a divine revelation which opens one's eyes to a different and new vision of life. This new revelation leads to a radical change in the way of thinking and living. I chose to use the same concept to talk about social change in society at large.[2]

Many Christians with social concern seem to agree on the need for such a radical social change, but we do not know at the present conjuncture how and where to begin. The following reflection does not pretend to answer this question; it is rather a theological reflection which suggests some questions to help us initiate a discussion in our faith communities on our social reality in light of our Christian faith.

Like personal conversion, social conversion, I believe, has its source in God's committed love to all creation. It is also rooted in our faith in the Spirit of life at work in history. I see social conversion as the result of the interaction between divine grace and human history through our faith; it is a concrete acceptance of God's gift of life and love, and a denouncement of any action, structure or process which degrade life and the dignity of creation.

I propose the following questions to initiate a theological reflection on social conversion:

(1) How do we talk about God's presence in our society, and about God's gratuitous love to all peoples and creation at the present global conjuncture?

(2) How do we talk about Jesus' project of the Reign of God, of love,

---

[2] Catholic Social Teaching, for example, uses the concept "structures of sin" to name the root of social evil. A system (political, economic, cultural etc.) becomes evil when it works against the common good, and especially when it excludes the less privileged members of society. The Encyclical "Social Concerns" calls for taking a radical attitude in order to confront and transform the social structures of sin, which the Papal document describes as being motivated by an "all-consuming desire for profit," and a "thirst for power" at any price. The Encyclical also calls for "a commitment to one's neighbour with the readiness to 'lose oneself' for the sake of the other instead of exploiting and oppressing the other for ones own advantage (Mt 10:40-42; 20:25; Mk10:42-45; Lk 22:25-27)" (Social Concerns, 38).

justice, and peace for us individually, for our community and for our world today? Where do we find witness in our society to the Reign of God? How do we name these witnesses? What does their witness have to say to us about our way of life?

(3) If continuing the project of Jesus to proclaim and build the Reign of God is the core message and mission of the believing community, how do we talk about this project today? How do we name this project in political, economic, cultural and ecological terms? How do we talk about Jesus' way of life, options, teaching, works, death and resurrection in relevant political, economic, cultural and ecological terms which make sense to us and to our society today?

(4) How do we name the work of the Spirit in our midst—locally and globally—at this moment in our history?

(5) How do we evoke a sense of ethical responsibility among the members of our faith communities so that we can make concrete options for the common good of all? How do we talk about global solidarity in concrete terms? What does it mean for us today to live in harmony with mother earth and the rest of God's creation?

Nurturing Our Vision and Spirituality

"For many of us," notes the Moderator of the United Church of Canada, "the issue is a spiritual one. What are human beings for? How do we view human community and the earth itself? Through what lens do we see the world and our place in it? It cannot be denied that we live in a time of severe disruption. And we cannot return to the packaged positions of the past. But is the future of the human community and of the earth itself to be determined by a pathological devotion to this global market whose so-called 'invisible hand' has no conscience?"[3]

Christians around the world are preparing to celebrate a Great Jubilee at the turn of the millennium. This could be a historic

---

[3] Bill Phipps, "An Invitation to Respond."

opportunity. A re-thinking of our social reality in light of God's love for all creation and faith in the Spirit of life alive in our midst, is an urgent call.

Faith in the resurrection and hope for our world continue to be affirmed today—as in the time of Jesus—by the most humble and the poorest among us; those who live at the margin of our society. These signs of hope existed in every society and they are present among us as well. Opening our eyes of faith to see the work of the Spirit on the margins of our world, and affirming the hope growing from these "marginal" initiatives could be a source of hope for all of God's creation. A collective affirmation of the genuine signs of hope emerging from the margins of society could be an opportunity for us to open our eyes to a broader social conversion.

During moments of crisis in history, we need particular wisdom to see and understand what is happening around us. It might not be a bad idea to remember what Jesus said about to whom God's wisdom is revealed and from whom it is hidden!

Michel Andraos is Ph.D. candidate at the Toronto School of Theology working on the Theology of Peace.

14

Good News to the Poor!
Background Paper on The Bible, Poverty, and
Government in Contemporary Canada

Evangelical Fellowship of Canada

Lord, when did we see you hungry and feed you,
or thirsty and give you something to drink?
When did we see you a stranger and invite you in,
or needing clothes and clothe you?
When did we see you sick or in prison and go to visit you?
(Matthew 25:37-39)

Introduction

J esus inaugurated his ministry (Lk 4:16-30) with a sermon on the
well-known Jubilee passage in Isaiah 61:2-3, which announces
good news to the poor, freedom for prisoners, sight for the blind,
release for the oppressed, and the coming of the year of Lord's favour. His startling claim that "today this scripture is fulfilled in your
hearing" led some of his home town listeners to try kill him! What
does Jesus' claim lead Christians to do as we enter the third millennium? How does Jesus' death and resurrection influence our hearing
of this passage? Will we proclaim good news to the poor in our time
and place?

This paper is a biblical primer on poverty, written to help contemporary Christians understand the importance of the Bible's message about poor neighbours. It does so by setting out a biblically-
based framework for understanding and acting on poverty in today's
society. This paper helps Christians see that the needs of poor people
at home and abroad are connected to the very heart of the Gospel. In
specific, this background paper aims to encourage dialogue in the

---

1 An EFC 'Position Paper' is one which has been officially endorsed by the Or
ganisation. An EFC 'Background paper' is a serious document, created by a Task

Christian community regarding contemporary poverty issues, to inform the Evangelical Fellowship of Canada's action in the public realm, to encourage local churches to serve the poor in our communities, to inspire Christians in all social roles—work, recreation, volunteering, investing, family, etc. to serve and empower the poor, and finally to encourage the state to do justice for the poor and eliminate the causes of poverty.

Who Are the Poor?

What makes a person or family poor in Canada, or for that matter, in any country? How can we recognise poverty when we earnestly seek to discern which of our neighbours are in need?

In Canadian society, poverty is commonly associated with scarcity of income and material resources. Statistics reveal some important material dimensions of poverty. In 1989, 14.1% of Canadians lived in poverty while in 1995, 17.8% of Canadians lived in poverty. Fully 21% of Canadian children lived in poverty in 1995 (Stats. Can. Income Dist. by Size, 1995). Well-meaning political words have not helped. Parliament unanimously resolved in 1989 to make significant strides towards the elimination of poverty among Canadian children. In spite of that resolution, today there are half a million more poor children in Canada than there were in 1989.

Many people share in poverty and crippling personal and national debts world-wide. In an era when globalisation is heralded as the means to achieve progress and prosperity for all, dire poverty plagues many around the world. The UN Development Program has discovered that 1.3 billion people lived on less than US $1 per day in 1997. Annually, twelve million children under the age of 5 die because of hunger and preventable diseases (UNICEF). And the spectre of poverty continues to grow in under-developed nations: in 1960 the poorest 20% of the world accounted for 2.3% of the world's economic activity, while the richest 20% accounted for 70.2%. In

Force or Commission to encourage dialogue within our community. This abridged version of the Background Paper has been produced by the Social Action Commission.

1993 this condition worsened to 1.4% for the poorest and 85% for the richest.

Statistics, however, are often hotly disputed. Christians frequently allow themselves to become entangled in debates about the validity of one or another set of statistics and fail to acknowledge that the flesh and blood people behind the numbers are "image-bearers of God." A good place to start making sense of this statistical debate is to ask what is meant by poverty. The Statistics Canada poverty line, for example, indicates that a family is likely to experience poverty when it spends 58.5% or more of its gross household income on food, shelter, and clothing. Although there may be good arguments to adjust the cutoff lines up or down, this definition of poverty is useful for giving us an indication of the number of people who are likely to experience the hardships of poverty. This definition is weak, however, in that it tends to reduce poverty to lack of finances.

Christians can improve on the statistical method of getting at the complex but hard hitting reality of poverty through the biblically based concept of calling. Christians sometimes limit their idea of calling to church- and evangelism-related ministries. Within God's creation, however, people are called to image and respond to God in a wide range of activities, e.g. people are called to nurture children, to work creatively, to care for neighbours, to play, and to steward the earth. In the broad setting of creation, these callings can be seen as opportunities to be faithful or unfaithful to God.

This broader understanding of calling leads to a more complex definition of poverty. Poverty exists when persons, associations or institutions lack the resources and space they need to fulfil their God-given responsibilities and callings. For example, a person or family might lack money but they may also lack skills, healthy habits, or enabling opportunity structures. One or another institution—like a school, hospital or farm—may lack the resources it needs to properly fulfil its functions in society. Furthermore, entire communities may become poor, for example, certain inner-city neighbourhoods, native reserves, or rural districts. Poverty weakens and undermines our capacity to 'open up' and tend creation as God originally intended us to do in His great benediction of Genesis 1:27-31. Understood in this way, poverty can never be a secondary concern for Christians since it strikes close to the heart of what it means for humans to image God.

This definition of poverty offers a variety of advantages. First, the main strength of this broader definition is that it helps show that poverty is as multi-dimensional as the human beings God created. People can be weakened in their ability to fulfil their callings for more reasons than simply the lack of material resources. People can become poor in social, economic, psychological, and spiritual ways. They can be family-poor, job-poor, friends-poor, food-poor, cash-poor, culture-poor, land-poor, etc. While poverty does not undermine our dependence on grace in Christ Jesus, it weakens our capacity to fully respond to the multi-dimensional callings in our daily lives.

A second advantage of this definition of poverty—as a lack of resources or space needed to fulfil a person's, association's or institution's God-given responsibilities and callings—is that it gives us a starting point for distinguishing "needs" from "wants." In contemporary economics, it is assumed that no one can make a valid distinction between needs and wants because they are both based on individual value choices and thus beyond moral criticism or external limitation. But if we understand that "needs" are directly related to the resources and space required to fulfil one's God-given callings, we acknowledge that there are standards external to the individual person that help us discern "enough." Importantly, as persons, institutions, and communities discern "need," we will also find that it is a two-edged sword, it not only helps us discover who is poor and needy, but also helps us know who in the community has abundance and can contribute more toward the common good. The resulting understanding gives Christians a basis for the stewardship of all of the gifts and resources with which we have been entrusted. Only when a society has a sense of enough—our real needs are being met—can it also develop a sense of "abundance" and thus appropriate thankfulness to God!

Third, the proposed definition of poverty also reminds us that we must discern who is poor in a context. People did not need the same types of resources and space to live their lives in 1000 AD as they do in 2000 AD, nor do people living in the inner city of Edmonton need the same resources and space as people living in a small farm in China. Time and place significantly influence how we define poverty and how people experience various forms of poverty.

Fourth, this definition acknowledges that the specific callings and/or responsibilities of people and institutions in society shape the type and amount of resources and space they need. As we publicly and politically address poverty, we need to be able to discern the nature of different callings and institutions in order to develop a sense of what they might require in order to fulfil their responsibilities.

Fifth, this definition of poverty recognises that the determination of callings, poverty, enough, need, wants, etc. will **always** involve human judgement—in response to God's word and creation—and can never be reduced to a particular Bible text, a mechanistic political or social formula, or a simple financial or statistical cutoff point for poverty. Poverty is a human, social, and relational reality; it concerns real people in a variety of offices and callings as they make real choices.

Adopting this multidimensional definition of poverty can also lead to new distortions; that is, we can be tempted to underestimate the importance of finances to the poor. People who exist in absolute poverty in our society may be able to survive physically, but is mere survival sufficient to fully respond to God in contemporary Canada? A family without any cash flow in present-day Canada simply cannot obtain the day-to-day necessities needed to fully respond to God's callings, e.g. they need cash for rent, groceries, bus fare, telephone, and clothes. For many people, falling back on a self-sufficient farm life is a faded dream and cash flow has become critical for fulfilling their callings in an urban society.

Poverty, Wealth and Idolatry

The problem of poverty is often attributed to irresponsible personal behaviour. This makes some sense in light of a multidimensional definition of poverty. A host of personal or family sins can initially trigger or exacerbate one's poverty. An important dimension of addressing poverty must be the community's urging that we each take some responsibly for our good and bad moral, consumption, employment, educational, and other choices. Some forms of poverty will have to be addressed in part on an interpersonal level, that is, by sitting down together with the people affected to discuss what has gone wrong and what needs to be done to set it right.

As important as personal responsibility may be in dealing with certain cases of poverty, however, there are a number of larger societal choices that we have made that also cause poverty. These choices notably fall within the power of many Canadian Christians to influence and change. Poverty is directly linked to "wealth" in so far as the poor often lack access to wealth as a means of fulfilling their callings. But, this is not to vilify wealth. The Bible portrays wealth and material things originally and ultimately as parts of God's good creation (Ge 1&2, Col 1:15-23). Material wealth and prosperity are often pictured in the Bible as gifts of God when they are used in the context of covenantal obedience to him (Dt. 8:18, Ecc 5:19, Jos 1:8, Ps 17:14). Material things are an integral part of the coming of shalom which the Bible declares God is eagerly bringing into the cosmos. The prophet Isaiah, for example, paints an eschatological picture in which "the wealth of nations" is brought into Jerusalem as a gift to God and his people (Is 60:11). This is echoed in Revelation 21:26 where the "glory and honour of the nations" are brought into the New Jerusalem.

The sharp paradox between our wealthy society and simultaneous poverty ought to signal to Christians the need to discern the "spirit of our times." Wealth, like any other created thing, can become twisted and oppressive in the hands of sinful human beings. Wealth is easily twisted by personal and social sins of greed, gluttony, and pride. Something spiritual goes wrong with wealth. The Bible uses the word idolatry to describe the major way that creaturely things can be twisted. It teaches that idolatry is the sinful human tendency to trust in a part of creation for provision and salvation rather than in the life-giving Creator.

Something as simple as the gift of daily bread can become an idol when we expect it to take care of our needs rather than waiting on God and his life-giving word, i.e. people "do not live by bread alone but by every word that comes from the mouth of God" (Mt 4:4, Lk 4:4, Dt 8:3). When a person, institution, or even an entire society desires wealth so strongly that they start trusting in the wealth-creation mechanisms of society—such as our jobs, businesses, or the market—to guarantee it, this misplaced trust transforms these things into idols.

The Bible refers to the idolatry of wealth as Mammon (Lk 16:13-15). The Bible further teaches that trust in material wealth and the market—in place of God—comes to nothing since idols are blind, deaf and dumb and can do nothing (Is 57:13; Ps 39:6-11, Hab 2:18-19). Ultimately, idolatry results in the opposite of what we expect, for we are converted into impotent and powerless people (Pm 115:8, 135:18, Gal 4: 8-9). And when idols make us powerless and ineffective, we not only hurt ourselves and our families, but as a society we can also seriously undermine our neighbours' wellbeing. This can be seen in the irony that our society acts like it is powerless to do anything about poverty while in fact we are one of richest societies ever in history! Idolatry leads us to produce "deceptive words" (Jer 7:3-8), or in modern terminology ideologies, that serve to allow us to call "evil good and good evil" (Is 5:20).

Christians sometimes think that they are exempt from idols. But closer inspection suggests that often we end up compartmentalizing our lives in such a way that pious service of God in private life coexists with some form of idol-worship in public. Jesus also explicitly warns us that "you cannot serve God and Mammon" (Lk 16:13-15). The idolatrous love of money is pictured as a stumbling block to following Jesus (Lk 14:33; 16:19-31). The record of the churches on domestic and international poverty give cause to reflect whether, and to what degree, idols and "deceptive words" may have influenced our lives.

Poverty and Grace

Christians often contrast "spiritual poverty" and "material poverty" and say that material poverty is secondary. This dualistic conception is not supported by the Bible. Scripture frequently refers to poverty and the poor so often that someone suggested that if you cut these

---

2 See Bob Goudzwaard, *Idols of our Time*, Dowers Grove, Illinois: IVP, 1984.

passages out of your Bible it would hang in tatters. In fact, the Bible portrays poverty and the poor—the widow, orphan, and stranger— within the larger drama of creation, the fall into sin, redemption through Jesus Christ, and the return of Christ. Within this redemptive story, possessions are pictured as part and parcel of fulfilling our God-given callings. The poor lack the resources, possessions, relationships and legal standing in the community needed to fully exercise their humanity through the exercise of their various callings and responsibilities in life. The Bible often pictures God standing over against sin and injustice and on the side of redemption and justice. God reveals himself as the liberator and restorer of sinful humanity, on the side of the poor, widow, and the orphan and against those who injure and oppress (e.g. Is 1:10-20, 3:13, 10:1-3, Pr 21:3, Mt 25).

Jesus' statement that "the poor you have with you always" (Mt 26:11) can be of great help in understanding the biblical message concerning the poor. This passage has been used by some Christians to suggest Jesus condones doing little or nothing for the poor. But this unbiblical emphasis misses the deeper thrust of the Gospel. Jesus borrows this phrase from the Old Testament passage which ends "therefore I command you to be open-handed towards your brothers [and sisters] and towards the poor and needy in the land" (Dt 15:11). Why? Because, the passage continues, "God will richly bless you in the land." This is God's grace! God had liberated Israel out of Egypt not because they deserved it but by grace (Dt 7:7). Once they were delivered into the Promised Land, the land of plenty, God gives Israel the opportunity to choose curses or blessings. He summons Israel to see their prosperity as the basis to care for others so that "there should be no poor" among them (Dt 15:4). God initiates redemption and provision, and the people are asked to respond to His generosity by caring for the poor.

Our understanding of Jesus' peculiar use of the phrase "the poor you have with you always" is deepened in the context of the Old Testament sabbatical laws. A sabbath year was to be observed every seventh year in which land was given rest—and whether one deserved it or not—debts were cancelled and servants set free (Lev 25, Dt 15). At the mathematical climax of the sabbath years (seven-times-seven years, or forty-nine years) came an additional Year of Jubilee. At the centre of the Year of Jubilee was the Day of Atonement when God pronounced the people cleansed of their sins. As a consequence of this pronouncement, the people were to "proclaim liberty throughout the land" (Lev. 25:8-12). Thus, at the very heart of God's early ordinances for Israel's social and economic order was the reality of unmerited forgiveness of sins or debts. So when we go back to Jesus' words "the poor you have with you always," we note that it ends with the phrase "but you will not always have me" (Mt 26:11). Jesus says this on his last journey to Jerusalem that ends with the cross. On the cross, Jesus fulfils the Day of Atonement once and for all. In the ultimate sense, Jesus' death and resurrection is the definitive Jubilee for all creation, it is the conclusive "good news to the poor," "freedom for the prisoner," "release for the oppressed," it is in fact "the year of the Lord's favour" (Lk 4:18-19, see Lk 7:21 and Mt 25:31).

In the Old Testament era, Israel was to function as a unique people pointing all the nations to the redemption that God was bringing into the world. The very structure of the economic, social, and political order that God set up for the Israelites in the sabbatical laws, points to the need for Jesus Christ. In Christ, we see God's love for the whole cosmos and his singular love for each person (Jn 3:16-17). Jesus is the solution for sin that lies at the heart of all human problems, including poverty in all of its dimensions. Grace in Jesus Christ works out from regenerated hearts into redeemed patterns of living, working, caring and sharing.

The biblical message of grace does not allow us to oppose soul against body, spiritual against material, and evangelism against justice. Redemption is integral to the whole of human existence. Thus, it should come as no surprise to New Testament believers that God's intention for human society as stated in Deut 15:4 is that "there should be no poor among you, for...he will richly bless you..." In fact, this message is echoed powerfully in the early practices of the New Testament church (Ac 2:42-47 and 4:32-35). The integrality of redemption is further evident in passages such as when John the baptizer sends his disciples to ask Jesus if he really is the Promised

One. Jesus replies "The blind receive sight, the lame walk, those who have leprosy are cured, the deaf hear, the dead are raised, and the good news is preached to the poor" (Mt 11:4-6). Shortly before Jesus entered Jerusalem for the final time, he told the parable in which he recognises his true followers as those who have fed the hungry, given drink to the thirsty, invited strangers in, clothed the naked, and visited the prisoner (Mt 25). Those who are restored to fellowship with God show this in every dimension of their lives.

The message of grace also does not allow us to oppose charity against justice. It is true that God called Israel to charity, that is, to be "open-handed" to the poor (Dt 15:8). But acts of charity were also to be structured into the very institutions and relationships of the new society in the Promised Land. These were to be societal structures of justice, that is, structures that routinely enabled the poor to achieve a full life within the community, for example, cancellation of debts (Dt 15:1), lending freely (Dt 15:8), returning land that was lost by the original owner (Lev. 25) and so on. These just societal structures allow the poor, the widow, and the dispossessed to be restored to full human and social participation.

Finally, the Bible does not allow us to treat justice for the poor as an optional frill over and above worship and evangelism. In fact, God emphatically warns us that worship and religion are empty if they are not accompanied by actions that come from a heart of gratitude and structures of justice and mercy (Is 1:10-20 & 58:3-12, Mt 23:23, Am 5:21-24, Hos 6:6, Mic 6:6-8, James 1:27, 2:17).

Spiritual Roots of Present-Day Poverty

The paradox we experience over the presence of scarcity in the midst of the continual and rapid growth of wealth in our country ought to alert us to something that has gone deeply wrong. Our society has achieved unprecedented **abundance** and incredible economic growth yet a sense of **scarcity** regularly surfaces in Canadian life in the forms of poverty, the pressure on funding for caring human services, and personal, corporate, and national debts. Canada's GDP grew constantly while our national debt simultaneously sky-rocketed. These paradoxical tensions between our wealthy society and personal and public scarcity beckon us to actively discern the "spirit of our times" (1 Jn 4:1) as it shapes our society and institutions.

Western civilisation has been shaped in part by ideologies of materialism, meritocracy, and statism. These ideologies are not neutral approaches to poverty and wealth which Christians can quietly adapt into their worldviews. In many ways, they are the antithesis of the biblical vision of free unmerited grace which we discussed above. Not only salvation from sin (Ro 3), but our life, food, breath, and shelter are gifts of God which he lavishes on both the sinner and saved (Mt 5:45, Job 25:3, Ps 145:9). Merit does not condition God's grace, or we would all immediately perish.

This is not to suggest that employees do not merit a just wage. Rather, the status of being human under God's creational and providential care means we should care for and share with all needy people. As the apostle John writes "if anyone has material possessions and sees his brother [or sister] in need but has no pity on him, how can the love of God be in him? Dear Children, let us not love with words or tongue but with actions and in truth" (1 Jn 3:16-17). Grace is founded on God's love and invites humanity to respond with lives based on love (Ro 13:8).

Ultimately, grace breaks the idolatrous powers of wealth, the market, or statism and places them back within the bounds of the Kingdom of God, making them servants of God's justice and shalom.

Poverty and Differentiated Society

Poverty should not be reduced simply to idolatry and spiritual failure on the part of society. Nor should the causes or solutions for poverty be interpreted narrowly as individual responsibility. Deep spiritual problems manifest themselves in highly complex societal structures. Poverty is deeply rooted in structures and practices that reflect a combination of sinful and healthy motives. It is tempting to look for quick and simple solutions, for example, by asking people to pick up their personal responsibilities, or by asking one particular institution—e.g. the state, church, or business—to solve poverty. But poverty cannot be addressed by passing the buck to the state, or simply requiring churches to do more for the poor, or demanding businesses create more jobs, or forcing individual persons to care for their neighbours.

Today' s society is a complex intertwinement of a variety of persons, institutions and relationships, often with their own unique differentiated responsibilities and rights. If we are going to ask what a particular Christian person should do about poverty, we need to understand how he or she is situated within our societal structures? **Who**—which people in which offices and institutions—should do **what** about particular instances of poverty?

The starting point for a Christian understanding of societal structures is the biblical message that God is the sovereign creator and sustainer of all things. All creaturely life, including human society and culture, is a **response** to the Lord of creation and history. This stands in stark contrast to many secular social and political theories that assume human society is invented and built by autonomous persons. These theories assume individual persons gather together to shape and create society as they will. Modern social institutions and relationships, therefore, are seen as the result of free creative choices rather than historical human responses to God's creational will for life. Adopting a biblical starting point leads us to reject notions of society that see it as an artificial construction that is totally malleable and remakeable.

We need to develop biblical wisdom in order to understand contemporary society. This requires that we continually reflect on the God-given nature of contemporary social institutions and offices in the light of scripture (Ps 119:105). Just as King Solomon, in his time and society, was able to discern the character of a faithful mother and so return the living child to its true mother (1 Ki 3:16-28), so in our society we must discern the character of various institutions and offices so we can give them their due.

As we analyse contemporary society, we immediately note that human responsibilities and rights are historically differentiating and unfolding, becoming located in a variety of distinct societal offices and institutions. For example, the entire society does not take direct responsibility for nurturing a child, parents do. All Canadians do not directly make choices about investment, rather bank managers, investors and others take the lead in these choices. Editors and news reporters take primary control of reporting, principals and teachers are responsible for teaching, farmers for farming, and pastors for preaching. The crucial point is that the character of our offices—including the nature of the institutions and associations within which one lives and works—shape, limit and condition our responsibilities and rights within society. The Bible implies this unfolding of society within creation when it pictures history moving from a "garden" to a "city" (Ge 1, Rev 21 & 22, Heb 11:16).

A helpful way of picturing society is to see it as a variety of differentiated institutions, associations, and persons that are closely interwoven and interrelated. These institutions and persons are not arranged vertically but horizontally—each one fulfilling its calling directly in relationship to God. No institution is responsible to God for the central calling and function of another institution, although the state and even the church have historically tried to claim that role. Business people are responsible to discern the will of God for their business practices and should not expect, nor allow, the state or church to dictate to them how they should act. The church and state do not have the overall competency to make these specialised types of choices. This is not to suggest that social, economic, and political institutions and associations ought to operate in isolation from one another. Rather, institutions and associations are responsible for mutually encouraging and admonishing one another to carry out faithfully their respective God-given callings.

An important correlate of the differentiation of social tasks is the reintegration of these entities. How should persons, families, hospitals, arts and drama groups, businesses, banks, internet companies, universities, schools, neighbourhood associations, media, brokerage firms, and other institutions relate together within one society? A good deal of social integration occurs directly through mutual discussion and accommodation between the various social players. The state, as we discuss later, has a special public role to play in legally enabling the just integration of society.

This unfolding of institutional responsibilities, as well as the re-integration of society, occurs either in obedience or disobedience to God. This yields societal practices and structures that reflect various degrees of health and brokenness. We only need to look around us to see that "the whole creation"—including the social and economic dimensions of human creatures—is "groaning as in the pains of childbirth." We know that "the creation itself will be liberated from bondage to decay and brought into the glorious freedom of the children of God" (Ro 8:22).

Viewing the responsibilities, both for causing and solving poverty, through the lens of a differentiated social structure has several benefits. First, it helps us understand that poverty is integrally linked to the proper functioning of the many components of society. Different people in a range of different offices need different kinds of resources. Second, each differentiated institution and office has its own unique and important contribution to make in fighting poverty. No matter which offices we function within, there are things we can do in these roles to address poverty. For example, journalists can report on the causes, extent and solutions for poverty, business people can address employment issues, and schools can help address poverty and learning. Whatever the unique task may be of each institution, however, they should all make sure that they wisely sustain life, enable the reversal of the cycle of poverty, and help prevent further poverty.

The church can also play an important role in fighting poverty. The church can be considered broadly as the "people of God" as they function in their every day lives and more narrowly as a specialised church "institution."

The church understood as "the people of God" functions in the full range of tasks and callings that make up modern differentiated society—e.g. Christians form families to nurture children, participate

---

[3] For articles dealing with a variety of societal actors and poverty, see Stanley Carlson Thies and James W. Skillen, Eds, *Welfare in America: Christian Perspectives on a Policy in Crisis*, Grand Rapids, MI: Eerdmans, 1996.

in schools to form minds of students, create businesses to produce useful goods and services, and so forth. As followers of Christ, we are invited to carry out these tasks and callings in love of God and neighbour and to actively oppose sinful ways of doing them. The church as the people of God can work within each of our everyday offices and callings in society to prevent and heal poverty.

The church, understood as a specialised and distinctive "institution" within the larger society, is the place where believers worship, preach, and engage in certain forms of direct service. The church understood in this sense can play a decisive and direct role in dealing with poverty. Many institutional churches could begin working on poverty by confessing frequent failure to bring "good news to the poor." Churches have often failed to enfold the stories of the poor and marginalized into the great encompassing story of God's redemptive love for the world. Beside the obvious importance of beginning to recognise the breadth of the Gospel, however, this would also allow the poor to be fully included in the local church. Inclusion is itself an important aspect of overcoming poverty. This would also give churches the opportunity to benefit from the contributions and gifts of the poor themselves.

The church as institution could specifically do the following:

(a) be prophetically bold in proclaiming God's call to do justice and fight oppression in our country and abroad (even when this involves people in our own pews),

(b) help Christians recognize that everyone is needy and so as recipients of God's abundance we are called to be givers,

(c) pursue thoughtful and empowering initiatives to benefit the poor in the church neighbourhood,

(d) in appropriate ways, encourage and promote community actions and public policies that help bring meaningful relief to the poor, and

(e) become more knowledgeable about the effects of international poverty on people—including on brothers and sisters

---

[4] A helpful model for understanding differentiated responsibilities and poverty is "Charter of Social Rights and Responsibilities" developed by Citizens for Public Justice.

in Christ abroad—and actively participate in international relief, development, and justice organisations.

The State's Role in Fighting Poverty

Canadian churches have publicly addressed the government's role in addressing poverty in society, although sometimes in conflicting ways. Some churches push government to do more while others ask it to do less. The definitions of the task of government used by the various churches are never neutral, that is, they intrinsically reflect a religious or ideological vision of life. Since all institutions in society should mutually encourage and admonish one another to properly fulfil their respective callings, churches need to speak out—not only to Christians exercising their various offices in society—but also to society-at-large and the state. This final section is a contribution to the ongoing reflection Christians need to do on the character of the modern state's task in the light of Scripture.

A clearer understanding of the distinctive character and calling of the state will allow Christians to speak more effectively to the state's role in dealing with poverty.

In the letter to the church in Rome, the heartland of the great Roman Empire, Paul calls the governing authorities "God's servants" (Ro 13:1-7)! He describes government's task negatively as punishing evil and positively as being "God's servant to do you good." Paul clearly does not mean that government is called to usher in the Kingdom of God or that it has the overarching task of enforcing true religion in society. Government is not called to do everything in society. But neither is the state cut off from God's rule as some Christians might conclude from the passage "Give unto Caesar what is Caesar's and to God what is God's" (Mk 12:13-17). In this passage, Jesus exposes the "hypocrisy" of Pharisees who want to trap Jesus by playing God off against a deified Caesar. Jesus condones paying taxes to Caesar precisely because even the mighty Emperor can only func-

---

5 For a helpful discussion of Christian social and political responsibility see Brian C. Stiller, *From the Tower of Babel to Parliament Hill: How to be Christian in Canada Today.* Toronto: Harper Collins, 1997.

tion as government under the sovereign rule of God. The task which is Caesar's comes from and belongs to God!

Within the highly differentiated structure of contemporary Canadian society, therefore, the state has a distinct and limited responsibility before God. In the Old Testament, this task is frequently described as doing justice (e.g. Ps 72, 82). But what does justice entail in our modern differentiated society? Clearly the state does not have the competency to enact justice in every societal situation, e.g. justice in family relations, in business pay scales, or classroom conflicts. Since government plays a restricted role in achieving the full reality of biblical justice, it is important to delimit the modern state's task to doing 'public justice'.

But what does a state actually "do," what functions does it perform, when seeking to do public justice in society? As social responsibilities historically differentiate into specific institutions and offices they also need to be re-integrated into harmonious societal unity. Much of this is accomplished through mutual accommodation and negotiation between various persons, institutions and associations. A central function of government, however, is to set out a public legal order that can serve to justly integrate all social institutions together into one society according to public justice, that is, in a way that respects, enables and enhances their specific callings. Sometimes the state sets conditions which shape the future integration of society and sometimes the state follows up existing integration in order to correct distortions and oppression. Both are valid elements of government's public legal integration of society.

The state's task, however, includes more than simply making laws and regulations. Governments that legally integrate society may have to step in to prevent the oppression of one institution by another, intervene to justly reconstitute a distorted societal relationship, act to fulfil a particular function or service that is absent or failing, or arbitrate in order to restore a person or institution to its proper place when another institution unjustly absorbs its calling.

It is tempting to adopt a definition of the state's role that is static, or outlines a rigid set of do's and don'ts for the state, out of fear for the state's power and control. Christians have often been tempted to adopt the philosophical liberal trap of drawing an impermeable wall of separation between the state and other social institutions. This approach, however, leaves us trapped in a mechanistic understanding of society and human responsibility. The callings of societal institutions are unique and limited but they are also dynamic callings from God. Government, along with all social actors, is admonished to "let justice roll on like a river, righteousness like a never-failing stream" (Am 5:21-24). This metaphor suggests a dynamic and insistent effort to walk justly with God and our neighbour in the daily circumstances of our society.

In relationship to the poor, government ought to ensure that a satisfactory supply of housing, food, clothing and income is accessible to the needy; it should empower the initiative and exercise of responsibility by poor persons, institutions, and neighbourhoods; and government should promote initiatives that help business, unions, and other groups create employment for the poor. While poverty programs should appeal to and activate the God-given responsibilities of people and institutions, these initiatives should in the deepest sense be motivated by **grace**—the unmerited economic and social "new start" for all (Dt 15, Lev. 25, Mt. 25). For Christians, public justice for the poor is also firmly rooted in the cross of Jesus.

Finally, the state has the right to tax citizens in order to fulfil its calling (Ro 13:5-7). The adequacy or fairness of various taxes needs to be judged in the context of the task of government and the demands of justice in our society at particular times and in specific places.

Conclusion

Jesus' startling message that the Year of the Lord's Favour includes good news for the poor is a wonderful, third-millennium challenge for today's church. Some Christians may respond to this message with hopelessness and surrender because of the immense scope and gravity of poverty in Canada and around the world. We need to remember, however, that Jesus also said "today this scripture is fulfilled in your hearing." In Jesus Christ the ultimate victory over sin and evil has already been won. God has already gone ahead and initiated his

Kingdom of righteousness and justice. It does not ultimately depend on our work and efforts. The Holy Spirit is beckoning and empowering us to be faithful and to gratefully respond to God's work in our everyday callings. In this way, we are becoming "letters from Christ... written not with ink but the Spirit of the living God" (2 Co 3:3). And as open letters, our neighbours will be able to read in us the concrete reality of good news for the poor, freedom for prisoners, sight for the blind, release for the oppressed, and the coming of the year of the Lord's favour (Lk 4:16-30).

Approved 26 August 1999: abridged Sept. 1999.

15

Loosening the Cords that Bind Us: Reflections on a Theology of Debt

Mark Hathaway

The call to cancel debt, especially the debts of the poor, lies at the heart of the biblical Sabbath and Jubilee years. Both freedom from debt and freedom from the forms of slavery that resulted from indebtedness were seen as essential conditions for an authentic liberation. Indeed, the release envisioned by both Sabbath and Jubilee went beyond the cancellation of debts and the emancipation from servitude. When slaves were freed during the Sabbath year, they were to be given a fresh start in life including adequate provisions of food, wine, and livestock (Deut. 15:12-14). The Jubilee went even further, returning lands (that had often been sold to pay debts) to their ancestral owners, ensuring a sound foundation for a dignified livelihood (Lev. 25:13-17).

The relevance of these traditions today may be even greater than in the time of ancient Israel. We live in a world where the majority of nations are trapped by an ever-growing mountain of debt—a debt they can never hope to repay under current conditions. To make matters worse, creditors have imposed harsh austerity measures called "Structural Adjustment Programmes" (and indeed, an entire economic model) on debtor nations, often as a condition for receiving new loans to pay interest on the old. Debt now sentences whole countries to a form of virtual enslavement characterised by a loss of economic sovereignty and the impoverishment of entire peoples. Indeed, on deeper analysis, we could say that debt has become a system of entanglement that traps the entire Earth community in its web – it threatens to impoverish us all by destroying the Earth's true wealth and beauty.

How can we free ourselves from the cords of debt, "Structural Adjustment," and the destructive economic system they sustain? In order to search for insights into these questions, we will first look at the call to loosen the bonds of debt that lies at the very heart of the prayer that Jesus taught us. Then, we will look at parallels between this call and the teachings of the Jubilee and Sabbath traditions. Using these insights, we will then examine the modern situation of international debt in its multiple dimensions.

A Point of Entry: The Lord's Prayer

Most of us are well aware that there are two, slightly different versions of the prayer Jesus taught us—one found in Luke (11:2-4) and the other in Matthew (6:9-13). While the version in common usage more closely resembles Matthew's, it opts for Luke's phrasing on the line "Forgive us our sins/trespasses (vs. Matthew's "debts") as we forgive those who sin against us." Actually, even Luke uses "debts" in the second half of the line. It is interesting to speculate, then, how the current wording became commonplace. Is it because we are more comfortable with the idea of forgiving sins than debts?

To look more deeply at this line, it is helpful to consider the Aramaic version[*] of Jesus' prayer drawing on the work of Neil Douglas-Klotz (1990, pp. 30-1). The phrase can be transliterated as:

Washboqlan khaubayn (wakhtahayn)
aykanna daph khnan shbwoqan l'khayyabyn.

(The text in parentheses is the word used in Luke's version of the prayer.)

Douglas-Klotz notes that the essence of this line is the idea of "letting go of past mistakes that tie ourselves and one another into knots." The key words in the text are:

- **shboqlan** ("forgive") meaning to return to its original state or re-establish slender ties. "The prayer reaffirms that our original state is clear and unburdened, one where the slender ties to creation are based on mutual releasing."
- **khaubayn** (Matthew) meaning debts, hidden past, secret debts, and hidden or stolen property.

---

[*] Found in the Peshitta version of the biblical texts used by many Eastern rite Christians.

- **khtahayn** (Luke) meaning failures, mistakes, accidental offences, frustrated hopes, tangled threads "the latter implying that some mending or restoration is needed."
- **aykanna** ("just as") implying that "releasing must be done consistently and regularly if our knotted relationships are to become whole and stable once again."

Meditation on these words can yield many fresh insights. To "forgive" means to re-establish ties, to re-create right-relationship. This is not a one-sided action. Mutuality seems to be implied. This is a release from threads that entangle a relationship. There is even a connotation here of "embracing with emptiness." It is a clearing, a renewal.

And what is being released and disentangled? Debts, yes; but also "hidden or stolen property." Note the idea of secrecy. Does this imply that debt is a subtle way of stealing, of usurping what is not really ours to take?

Luke's word, *khtahayn*, seems to have interesting implications as well. "Tangled threads" certainly is an evocative image when reflecting on debt, as is "frustrated hopes." The idea that we are called to mend something is also suggestive.

Aykanna carries a strong connotation of regularity, of consistency. Untying, release, forgiveness must be done on a regular basis if relationships are to be truly healed. We cannot think in terms of "once and for all." A regular cycle of release, untangling, and mending is needed.

Jesus' prayer makes no explicit reference to Jubilee or Sabbath, but similar principals seem to be involved. Jubilee and Sabbath call for society to "return to original state that is clear and unburdened" by slavery and debt. They call for a regular cycle of mending and re-establishing the ties of relationship with each other and to the Earth. The idea of returning "stolen property" is also echoed in the Jubilee's redistribution of land and the Sabbath's generous fresh start for those who had been enslaved.

Looking at Debt Today

What would untying the threads of past mistakes mean today? What would it mean to mend relationships destroyed by debt, to return hidden or stolen property to its rightful owners? In order to answer these questions, it is helpful to use the analysis of activists in Southern nations who point out that the massive debt their peoples bear is unpayable, illegitimate, and immoral (*The Tegucigalpa Declaration*).

The unpayability of the debt becomes quickly apparent by looking at some statistics. In 1980 the South's total debt stood at US $568 billion. Between 1980 and 1997 they paid out $2.9 trillion in interest and principal payments. Yet, their total debt now stands at $2 trillion! Each person in the South owes an average of US$300 to Northern creditors. African countries now pay four times more in debt payments than they do for healthcare (*A New Beginning*).

The case of Brazil, technically considered a "middle income" country, is instructive: In 1994, its debt stood at a US$ 148 billion. Since that time, it has paid over US$ 126 billion to foreign creditors, but its debt now stands at over US$ 270 billion (*Life before Debt*). Given the effect of rapidly accumulating interest, it is quickly evident that even a resource-rich nation like Brazil can never pay off its debt under current conditions.

•   •   •   •   •   •

It is also important, though, to recognise that the debt borne by poorer nations is largely the result of injustice on many levels, and is hence *illegitimate*. Much of the money originally loaned was borrowed by questionable regimes that were not chosen democratically (including military regimes and the apartheid regime in South Africa). Some was borrowed to buy arms used for repression, some for poorly thought-out mega-projects. Much was lost to corruption. What is clear in all these cases is that responsibility for these bad loans should be shared by the lenders, corporations, and local elites who reaped benefits from them. Yet, this is not what has happened; instead, the poor, who often suffered (and who seldom benefited) from the way the original loans were used, are those who are now forced to make sacrifices in order to pay.

The debt burden is also the result of unjustly high rates of interest that multiplied rapidly during the 70's and 80's. Once again, the increase in interest rates was outside the control of those who now bear the burden of repayment. In fact, the root of the dramatic rise in interests rates lay in the United State's decision to float the dollar in the early 70's, itself the result of the deficit spending used to finance the Vietnam war. As the dollar lost value, oil producing nations raised prices to compensate and an inflationary spiral set in. Monetarist economists then promoted high interest rates to dampen demand (i.e. induce recession). As a result, poorer nations saw the interest on their outstanding loans skyrocket (interest rose from 4 to 6 percent to over 20 percent in a matter of months at the end of the 70's). At the same time, the recession provoked by these policies depressed demand for Southern exports, commodity prices fell, and loans became even more difficult to repay.

In recent years, a series of financial crises, including those of Mexico and much of Asia, has further compounded this problem. In response to these crises, international financial institutions and wealthy creditor nations sponsored massive rescue packages (i.e. new loans) to "stabilise" economies thrown into chaos by economic liberalisation, but most of this money went into bailing out those involved in financial speculation. The common people of these nations are now being forced to pay for the cost of these new loans (from which, once again, they derive little or no benefit). Effectively, the poor are being required to transfer resources to wealthy investors.

•   •   •   •   •   •

Here we can see how the story of debt seems to mirror the image of entangled threads – threads of war, usury, corruption, greed, and speculation. Past mistakes and past injustices seem to multiply and the web of misery grows more and more complex. This is especially true when we consider what happened when creditors began to impose harsh austerity measures, normally called "Structural Adjustment Programmes" (SAPs), as a condition for extending further credit to highly indebted nations.

Ostensibly, SAPs are a series of economic "reforms" designed to control high inflation and to free up resources for debt repayment. Among their chief characteristics are currency devaluations, the reduction of subsidies and trade barriers, cuts to government services, rises in local interest rates, and the orientation of the economy toward the production of commodities for export. The net result of such measures includes both higher unemployment and increases in the price of essentials like food, utilities, and health services. SAPs, then, shift the cost of debt onto the shoulders of the poor, particularly those of women and children.

SAPs also accelerate the destruction of ecosystems as economies shift to the production of new exports that will earn foreign currency needed for debt payments. For example:

- Forests are rapidly felled for lumber exports, destroying biological diversity and eventually converting vast tracts of land into virtual desert.
- As export crops take over the best land, peasants are pushed into farming steep hillsides vulnerable to soil erosion. At the same time, pesticide and chemical fertiliser use increases.
- Shrimp farming destroys mangrove swamps and makes coastal areas more vulnerable to flooding.

•   •   •   •   •   •

Beyond "freeing resources" for debt repayment, the main objective of SAPs seems to be to create a cheap pool of labour desperate for jobs, generate cheap exports of raw materials for international markets, and open new markets to Transnational Corporations. Nicaraguan economist Xabier Gorostiaga describes SAPs as a "new means of maintaining a straightjacket of political and economic control" over the South (*Nicaragua: Releasing a people...*). Essentially, SAPs are a tool for imposing what is sometimes referred to as "neo-liberal economics" — a model of savage capitalism that sacrifices the well-being of the vast majority of humanity as well as the wider Earth community to enrich a few. We could also call this model "corporate global-isation" or even "global corporatisation" because it basically moulds the economy in such a way as to ensure greater corporate dominance and profitability in the world economy.

In reflecting on this situation, the idea in Jesus' prayer of "frustrated hopes" comes to mind: the frustrated hopes of a mother whose child dies because of cuts to healthcare, the frustrated hopes of youth who cannot get a good education or find a job, the frustrated hopes of entire peoples reduced to a struggle for survival – unable to use their gifts for the creation of beauty and the healing of the Earth community.

Moreover, what is clear is that debt has been used to construct a new form of economic slavery in the world, something that is fundamentally *immoral*. People, other creatures, and the Earth itself are being consumed to maintain the flow of debt payments. Yet, the debt grows ever greater and the prospect of ever being free from its burden seems at best a distant dream for the huge majority of the world.

It is important to note that those of us in the North have also suffered as a result of debt – particularly the poorest sectors of our own society. The cuts in social programmes and the growing impoverishment of children in Canada point to the price we have paid in the "battle" of deficit reduction. Here, too, debt was largely the result of the combination high interest rates and tax cuts to the wealthy that benefited only a small minority.

At the same time, though, many of us have also benefited from the suffering which debt has caused in the South. We pay far less than is just for many products because of the cheap labour and commodity prices induced by SAPs. Our way of life is being subsidised by the suffering of the poor and the suffering of the creatures who share the Earth with us.

Who Owes What to Whom?

People in the North tend to think of the debt crisis as a crisis of poor people who cannot repay what they borrowed. In Nicaragua, we see the debt crisis in a different way. The problem of debt is part of a larger chain of problems including the unfair terms of trade that pushed our governments to borrow in order to survive. We are unable to develop. (Carlos Pacheco, Nicaraguan Jubilee 2000 Campaign)

When we speak of cancelling debt, then, we must be clear that we are not talking about a question of "forgiving" loans. The tangled threads of debt, Structural Adjustment, and neo-liberal economics were woven by Northern governments, corporations, and financial institutions. It is now time for the North to make restitution to the poor and to the Earth itself.

Obviously, many people in the North were not directly responsible for these policies (resonating with the idea of "accidental offences" in Jesus' prayer). Yet, may of us have benefited in some form. Therefore, it is time that *we* ask for forgiveness. It is time for us to seek ways to begin to untangle the web of enslavement and destruction that ensnares us all.

This becomes even clearer if we take an historical view. What of the historical debt owed to Africa who saw its people lost to slavery? What of the gold and riches pillaged from the Americas (including the richness of natural wonders which have been forever lost)?

Guatemalan indigenous leader Guaicaipuro Cuautemoc illustrates this point by taking the example of the gold and silver taken from the Americas:

Between 1503 and 1660 alone, 185,000 kilos of gold and 16 million kilos of silver were shipped into San Lucar de Barrameda from America.

Plunder? I wouldn't say so. Because that would mean that our Christian brothers are violating their seventh commandment. Pillage? May Tanatzin have mercy on me for thinking that the Europeans, like Cain, kill and then deny their brother's blood! Genocide? That would mean giving credit to slanderers like Bartolomé de las Casas who equated the discovery of the Indies with its destruction, or to extremists such as Dr Arturo Pietri, who states that the outburst of capitalism and of the current European civilisation was due to the flood of precious metals! No way!

Those 185,000 kilos of gold and 16 million kilos of silver must be considered as the first of several friendly loans granted by

America for Europe's development. The contrary would presuppose war crimes, which would mean not only demanding immediate return, but also compensation for damage

I prefer to believe in the least offensive hypothesis. Such fabulous capital exports were nothing short of the beginning of a Marshalltezuma Plan to guarantee the reconstruction of a barbarian Europe, ruined by deplorable wars against the Muslim foe...

Financially, they were incapable—even after a moratorium of 500 years—of either paying back capital with interest or of becoming independent from net returns, raw material and cheap energy that they import from the Third World.

This disgusting picture corroborates Milton Friedman's assertion that a subsidised economy can never function properly, and compels us to claim—for their own good—the repayment of capital and interest which we have so generously delayed all these centuries.

Stating this, we want to make clear that we will refrain from charging our European brothers the despicable and blood-thirsty floating rates of 20 or even 30% that they charge to Third World countries. We shall only demand the devolution of all precious metals advanced, plus a modest fixed annum accumulated over 300 years.

On this basis, and applying the European formula of compound interest, we inform our discoverers that they only owe us, as a first payment against the debt, a mass of 185,000 kilos of gold and 16 million kilos of silver, both raised to the power of 300. This equals a figure that would need over 300 digits to put it down on paper and whose weight fully exceeds that of the planet Earth.

What huge piles of gold and silver! How much would they weigh when calculated in blood? To say that in half a millennium Europe has not been able to produce sufficient wealth to pay back this modest interest is as much as admitting to the total financial failure of capitalism. (TWN Features)

Humour aside, this quote clearly demonstrates the insidious nature of debt and compound interest. It also clarifies that, whatever fantastic sums the South supposedly owes to the North, it pales in comparison with what the North owes the South. Even limiting ourselves to recent decades, it is clear that both debt payments and unfair terms of trade have transferred an immense quantity of wealth from the poorer nations to the richer ones. (For every dollar currently going to the South in the form of aid, for example, three dollars returns to the North in the form of debt payments.) Establishing right relationship between North and South requires that the wealth the North has usurped (or stolen) from the South be returned. We cannot address the question of debt, then, without also addressing the question of redistribution of wealth.

Borrowing from the Earth, Impoverishing the Future

Adopting an ecological perspective adds further insights into the entangled threads that debt has woven in our world. As Guaicaipuro Cuautemoc's quote demonstrates, the very nature of compound interest means that debt spirals out of control exponentially. In this way, debt is fundamentally different from real wealth, which over time tends to either rot (like grain in silos) or remain constant (like gold in a vault). At its very best, wealth can grow at the rate of natural regeneration (like a forest), something that is limited by the fixed rate at which sunlight is absorbed and by other ecological boundaries. From an ecological view, it is inconceivable that wealth can grow exponentially over any extended period of time.

Herein lies the problem. As economist Herman Daly points out, debt is essentially a kind of lien against future production, a way of borrowing from the future. Since debt grows exponentially, production must also try to keep pace. The economic "pie" must keep growing just to keep up with interest. Even many "progressive" economists accept this idea, prescribing growth as a cure to economic ills. Note, for example that the Canadian Alternative Federal Budget has promoted higher growth to allow us to "outgrow" the deficit.

Yet, economies cannot grow indefinitely†. The human economy is a subset of the greater economy, the Earth's ecosystem. Already,

---

† For a more detailed discussion of ecological economics and the limits to growth, see "Rethinking Oikonomia: Ecological Perspectives on Economics" by Mark

we are approaching the limits of growth. The 20 richest percent of the world already uses 100% of its sustainable output, while the remaining 80% uses a further 30% (and both of these are very conservative estimates!). Hence, we are already in a state of "overshooting" the boundaries of sustainability. Indeed, humans now appropriate nearly half of the land-based "Net Primary Production"—the usable energy captured through photosynthesis from the sun. In another 20 years, we may take more than 80%. Clearly, indefinite growth is impossible. In fact, the stresses on the world's ecological health have already reached a point where much of the damage done is irreparable. Between 20,000 and 100,000 species—unique manifestations of the creativity of God—are now being lost each year. We are in very real danger of moving into a state of ecological collapse within the next few decades. We should remember the warning of Leviticus 26:34, that if the Earth is not given its due, it will "make up through desolation the years of Sabbath denied it."

●   ●   ●   ●   ●   ●

In theory, capitalism has at least a partial fix to the problem of ecological limits. As materials like wood, minerals, or petroleum become scarce, their price should rise and people should conserve and/or find more sustainable alternatives. This has not happened to any great degree, however, due to the implementation of SAPs: Poorer nations have been forced to produce more and more commodities for export (to earn cash for debt repayment), even if this means liquidating their last forests or farming on steep hillsides where erosion threatens to destroy soil forever. Labour costs, too, keep falling in the global race to the bottom, also keeping prices down. As a result, the price of commodities has remained stable, or even fallen. Essentially, though, the crisis has simply been delayed. By the time prices actually rise to reflect the true scarcity of resources, many ecosystems are likely to have been damaged beyond repair.

Hathaway posted on the Website of the United Church of Canada's Moderator's Consultation on Faith and the Economy [http://www.faith-and-the economy.org/Thm5Pap1-Oikonomia.htm].

• • • • • •

In essence, our current situation is one where we are destroying the "natural capital" of the Earth in order to satisfy the demand to accumulate the monetary capital needed to pay the compound interest owed on debt. We give priority to what is basically a purely human construct—interest on debt—over the very real limits of the Earth; but as Herman Daly has remarked, "there is something fundamentally wrong in treating the Earth as if it were a business liquidation." We are destroying the beauty and riches of the Earth, converting life into dead "capital." In David Korten's words, this is a case of "money colonising life." The unholy trinity of debt, SAPs, and neoliberal economics is at the heart of this trend.

The idea of "hidden debts" or "stolen property" seems very appropriate in reflecting on this situation. We have created an immense and very real debt to the wider Earth community to subsidise the lifestyle of a very small proportion of humanity. We are also borrowing from the future itself, undermining the ability of the Earth's ecosystems to sustain life. Once again, merely asking for forgiveness is not enough. We must find a way to disentangle ourselves from the web that traps us in a death-grip.

Loosening the Cords that Bind Us

What, then, must we do to loosen the cords that bind us?

First, we must embark on a process to cancel the debts of the South—including those of so-called "middle-income" nations. Yet, such a debt cancellation is really just a preparatory step to disentangling the bonds of injustice that impoverish the majority of humanity and the greater Earth community. We must also renounce the policies imbedded in SAPs and move away from corporate-led globalisation. Too, we need to respond to the deeper questions of returning the wealth that has been stolen from the poor though injustice.

Let us remember the idea that "releasing must be done consistently and regularly if our knotted relationships are to become whole and stable once again" (Douglas-Klotz). A healthy world order will require a structured process for cancelling onerous debts and preventing the build-up of such debts in the future. Indeed, we need to rethink the very convention of compound interest—at the very least, placing strict limits on the rate of interest that can be charged. Ultimately, if we are truly to unknot our twisted relationships, a new way of structuring our economy is essential. We need to create an economy based on the values of justice, equity, and sustainability.

Re-establishing right relationship with the rest of creation will mean that we must also address the often-hidden debt owed to the Earth itself; we must return to the wider community of creation that which we have forcibly usurped. We need to focus our creativity and resources on the healing of our planet.

Finally, we need to reflect on an entire spirituality of release. What does it mean to consistently untie the threads of past mistakes, return what has been stolen, and mend our relationship with the poor and with the Earth? Certainly, the concrete steps outlines above. Ultimately, though, we are called to radical conversion, a new way of understanding the very role of humanity our common household, the Earth. This entails finding meaning, not in acquisition and accumulation (almost the diametrical opposites of release!), but in sharing, celebration, and creativity. It means renouncing an ethic of domination and moving toward another based on cooperation with the natural processes of our planet. In so doing, we shall seek to create a world that "is clear and unburdened, one where the slender ties to creation are based on mutual releasing" (Douglas-Klotz).

Mark Hathaway, M.Ed. is a freelance "ecologian" who specialises in the intersecting concerns of ecology, economics, cosmology, spirituality, and theology. He writes, facilitates workshops and retreats, and designs Websites related to his areas of expertise. For more information, see http://www.visioncraft.org/.

References

A New Beginning: A Call for Jubilee (1998). The Vision of the Canadian Ecumenical Jubilee Initiative. [Posted to the Internet on the Website of the Canadian Ecumenical Jubilee Initiative at http://www.web.net/~jubilee/English/vision/index.html]

Cuautemoc, Guaicaipuro (~1996). "The Real Foreign Debt." Third World Network Features. [Posted to the Internet on the CEJI Website at http://www.web.net/~jubilee/English/articles/RealDebt(TWN).htm]

Daly, Herman E. (1996). *Beyond Growth: The Economics of Sustainable Development.* Boston: Beacon Press.

Douglas-Klotz, Neil (1990). *Prayers of the Cosmos: Meditation on the Aramaic words of Jesus.* San Francisco: Harper & Row.

Korten, David (1995). *When Corporations Rule the World.* West Hartford, Connecticut: Kumarian Press.

Life above debt: The verdict of Brazil's foreign debt tribunal. (April 1999). [Posted to the Internet on the CEJI Website at http://www.web.net/~jubilee/English/international/BrazilDebtTribunal(Ap99).htm]

"Nicaragua: Releasing a people from the bondage of debt and Structural Adjustment." *ALERTA,* No. 1 &2, 1999. (Toronto: Inter-Church Committee on Human Rights in Latin America)

The Tegucigalpa declaration: Yes to life, no to debt. (January 1999) [Posted to the Internet on the CEJI Website at: www.web.net/~jubilee/English/international/TegucigalpaDeclaration(Ja99).htm]

16

To Call the Sabbath a Delight
Lesbian and Gay Pride in the Jubilee Tradition

Lionel Ketola

Luke tells us, in his Gospel story,
that Jesus walked into his hometown synagogue in Nazareth,
where he grew up;
opened the Torah Scroll,
read the words of Isaiah 61 which we heard this morning:

"The Spirit of God is upon me
because God has anointed me to bring good news to the poor
to let the oppressed go free
to proclaim the Year of the Sovereign Ones favour" (Isa 61.1-2a)

and then concluded:
"Today, in your hearing, this scripture has been fulfilled."
The Sabbath Peace of the community erupts.
Jesus is thrown out of the synagogue.

Now while I'm willing to concede
that beginning with the story of an expulsion
might not be usual fare for a Lesbian and Gay Pride Homily,
when Jesus read this prophetic announcement from the scriptures
Jesus was not only implying that his embodiment of God's reign
was in reality an enacted announcement of Jubilee;
He was also indicting the social structures and forms of unjust
relationship of his day—
and making the claim
that only a call to Jubilee could
bring God's justice to bear on the situation.
Hence the expulsion.

The Jubilee tradition which Jesus was invoking
is a theology of liberation originating in the Hebrew Scriptures,
rooted in the central metaphor of Sabbath Rest.

Just as the Sabbath marked the cycle of the week
with a day of rest and recreation in community,
the Jubilee Tradition called for the observance of a yearlong sabbath
for the land.

Observing this sabbath rest of the land
meant to be confronted with the experience
of interconnection in a radically new way.

To let the land rest
was to see it as powerfully sacred
holding and sustaining
a diversity of living ecosystems.

To let the land rest was to acknowledge human reliance;
human labour, social relationships —
all of these start with the land and rely on its well being.

But the Jubilee Tradition went further,
stipulating that the Jubilee Year of Sabbath Rest
was also meant for the people, created from the soils of the earth.

By extending Shavat Shalom, the call to Sabbath Peace,
to the web of human relationships,
the whole community in all of its diversity
was drawn into the experience
of being freed up for Sabbath observance in community.

In order to accomplish this,
the Jubilee Tradition proclaimed and enacted 'a time apart'—
a time of literally restructuring economic and social relationships,
giving the community a concretely different shape,
restoring all of its members to a place
where they could once again fully and equally participate as citizens
in its social and economic life.
A time in which all of the community's members,
freed from the burdens of poverty and inequity,

could once again enjoy the fullness of Sabbath Rest, and in the words
of Isaiah:
"Call the Sabbath a delight,
and the Holy Day of God honourable"(Isa 58.13).

In the context of this vision of Jubilee,
this calling to interconnection and Sabbath Peace,
Maria Harris, in her recent work[1] on the spirituality of Jubilee,
raises the question of how it is that our own Sabbath Practices
have often been experiences of impoverishment
instead of embodiments of wholeness and Sabbath Delight.

Maria Harris suggests that our diminished experience
of Communal Celebration and Sabbath Peace
is the result of something which she identifies as:
"missing community,"
our continued separation from one another
our diminished sense of communal wholeness
maintained by structured forms of unjust relating.

This experience of what Harris has called: "missing community"
has been symbolised well, I think,
through some of our Parish community's experiences of the
Good Friday Liturgy.
(At The Church of the Holy Trinity, Toronto, ON.)

On Good Friday, we have often re-arranged the worship space
so that entire community is seated against the south sanctuary wall
in a long stretch of pews
which face into the centre of the worship space.

With this seating arrangement
the worshippers are confronted with the experience

---

[1] Maria Harris, *Proclaim Jubilee! A Spirituality for the Twenty-First Century* (Louisville, Kentucky: Westminster John Knox Press, 1996).

of being seated facing into a large empty space.
An emptiness
able to hold our Good Friday Intercessory Prayers
for the disappeared, the silenced, the displaced;
An emptiness
calling even the church
to consider its own sins of omission.

The task of holding this emptiness
while at the same time moving forward in our justice work as a
community
only seems possible
as we continue to value the significance and subversiveness of
storytelling—
not only as a resource for doing theology
but also as an action around which we can gather as a community
especially in those moments when our journeys seem most uncertain.

As such,
the stories which we heard told earlier this morning
recalling our Parish's history of welcome
toward Toronto's lesbian and gay community
are joined with many other strands of our community's
historical memory;
stories to root us and even question us as a community.

In another sense,
moving forward in our social justice work might involve
deepening our awareness of our community's own diversity,
exploring ways in which our community isn't able to hold or reflect
diversity,
and in the midst of this,
continuing in our commitments to solidarity
even when diverse visions of justice seem to intersect
and challenge all of our assumptions (about everything!).

So despite all of our questions and uncertainties

it seems we're continually learning as a community
to be more willing to risk testing
and standing on the strength of our commitments.

And even though the messages we're still receiving from
the larger church
would suggest that the price for sexual justice is too high;
that there really is no pay off for "giving a mere cup of water
to one of the most insignificant of these" (Mt 10.42),
we've come to believe as a community that *the opposite* is true:
—that we have more to lose when we don't stand for what we
believe;
—that Sabbath observances which only embody
what Maria Harris has called: "Incomplete Ecclesia" are not enough;
—that we want more,
—and that we are willing to take a stand for more.

Having said this,
our congregation's "Statement of Welcome,"
which we heard read this morning,
is an invitation to join us
in what Carolyn McDade would call: "the best of struggles;"[2]
an articulation of a hope
that as we walk in solidarity with all marginalized people,
we might know, once again,
the wholeness and delight of Sabbath Peace.

So struggle we will,
But today, being our Sabbath, we get to rest.
And today, being Lesbian and Gay Pride Day,
we invite you to join us in solidarity for a Parade—
as we celebrate Sabbath Delight and re-create ourselves as a
community;
as we claim for ourselves and for each other a foretaste of the Great

---

[2] Quoted from Carolyn McDade's song, *The Rest of Our Lives.*

Jubilee—where the yoke of injustice is removed;

where, in the words of Isaiah,
God's people receive "a garland instead of ashes,
the oil of gladness instead of mourning."
So in the words of that tradition:
Shavat Shalom!—and Happy Pride Day!

Homily for Lesbian and Gay Pride Day
The Church of the Holy Trinity
Sunday 27 June, 1999.

Lionel Ketola is a member of The Church of the Holy Trinity (Anglican), Toronto, Ontario.
A graduate (M.Div.) of the Lutheran Theological Seminary in Saskatoon, Saskatchewan,
Lionel currently works as an Expressive Arts Therapist in adult mental health.

17

Christian Faith and Globalization[1]

Jung Mo Sung

Social Apartheid

The major fact in the world's current environment is certainly the dreadful empire of the exclusion logic and the growing insensitivity of the great majority as regards exclusion.[2]

There are "poverty belts" not only in the so-called Third World countries but also in rich countries such as the United States. Such belts are created by those being excluded from the market, i.e., from decent life and even livelihood conditions. Being excluded from the market doesn't mean, however, being excluded from society and from the reach of the media that socializes the same consumer desires. Therefore, we are faced with a tragic situation where the poor are encouraged to desire consuming sophisticated and superfluous goods, while being denied access to the satisfaction of their basic survival needs.

One of the major causes of this exclusion process is certainly the structural unemployment impacting virtually the whole world. Current unemployment is referred to as structural because it is not an

---

[1] This article is a short version of the text "Fome de Deus, fome de pão, fome de humanidade" (Hunger for God, hunger for bread, hunger for humanity), presented at the Consultation of Missionary Boards of the NCCC-USA, in San Jose, Costa Rica, April/97. It also appears on the United Church of Canada Moderator's Consultation on Faith and the Economy website.

[2] Assmann, Hugo, "Por una sociedad donde quepan todos," in: Duque, José (ed), *Por una sociedad donde quepan todos*, San Jose (Costa Rica): Dei, 1996, 380.

environment situation resulting from an economic recession that could be overcome or mitigated with economic growth. On the contrary, large companies are making bigger profits and see their shares appreciate on stock exchanges, precisely because they are laying-off employees.

Structural unemployment is one of the fruits of the current global economy model and technological revolution. Both factors are creating such a global economy that, in the words of Peter Drucker, "production is no longer 'related' to employment, and capital movements, rather than trade (whether of goods or services), became the driving force of the global economy."[3]

This process may be seen as the climax of an inversion already described by Max Weber in his well-known book *Protestant Ethics and the Spirit of Capitalism:*

> [in Capitalism] man is dominated by money production, by acquisition, seen as the ultimate goal of life. Economic acquisition is no longer subordinated to man as a means to satisfy his material needs. This inversion of what could be called a natural relation, which is so irrational and naive, is clearly a principle that drives Capitalism.[4]

In the pre-modern societies, humans worked to survive. In Capitalist societies, people live to accumulate wealth. Currently, job cut programmes create more profit for companies and earnings for shareholders and executives. What's more, the financial system that should be connected to and at the service of the production system became bigger, more important and, to a great extent, disconnected from production. Wealth is financially-oriented and is largely "fictitious;" it no longer consists basically of tangible goods but rather of figures blinking on computer screens.

---

[3] Drucker, Peter, "As mudanças na economia mundial," *Política Externa* (Changes in the World Economy, *Foreign Policy*), vol.1., n.3, Dec/92, São Paulo: Paz e Terra, 17.

[4] Weber, Max, *A ética protestante e o espírito do capitalismo* (Protestant Ethics and the Spirit of Capitalism), 3rd. ed., S. Paulo: Liv. Pioneira, 1983, 33.

The problem is that such desire, such endless search for wealth for the sake of wealth, produces two very serious side effects. The first is the threat to the ecological system. The greed for more profit will eventually destroy an ecological system that took billions of years to be built and that makes human life possible. It also produces the severe social crisis striking our countries. Not only does it create poverty and social contrasts but also fast-growing violence and the increasing drug traffic and consumption.

Two other important factors should be mentioned for us to better understand the sad reality of Third World countries. The first is that being poor or jobless in a rich country where social programs really work is completely different from experiencing such a situation in countries that are dramatically cutting the budgets for existing scarce and inefficient social programs.

The second is that almost all Third World countries have what might be called "different overlapping times and spaces". In a single country, there are social groups living in different historic times. Some still live in a pre-modern culture, using production techniques of the agricultural revolution period, with no access to the formal education of industrialized urban societies. Others belong to the second technological revolution, the *Ford* industrial era, and still others live in a post-modern culture with access to last-generation technology. Such mismatch implies a serious economic and social problem. Many wish to work but are not qualified for the few jobs existing in the companies that require modernization owing to market pressures.

In addition, we have the serious problem of "space distance". The elite of our countries feels closer and more identified with the elite of rich countries than with the majority of our poor people. We might even say that the elite of our poor countries feels as if it belonged to the community of the world market consumers rather than to our domestic societies. In such a situation, it becomes much more difficult to obtain adhesion from the middle and upper classes to programs and policies that seek to solve our countries' social problems.

A Culture of Insensibility

A society which is based on an exclusion logic not only creates but is also fed by a culture of insensibility. Such virtually sceptical culture was neither born nor grows just by chance. It results from several historic and social factors and other factors of an anthropological nature. Owing to space limitation, we will only mention those factors which are more interesting to us.

Our societies nurture the idea that inequalities and social exclusion are inevitable. This concept gained prestige with the collapse of the Communist bloc. With the failure of that alternative model, the idea that Capitalism, with its neo-liberal ideology, represented the "end of history" (F. Fukuyama) gained momentum more than ever. With the dissemination of the concept that no other alternative is viable, our current social situation came to be seen as inevitable.

Not only inevitable but also fair. What Galbraith called "the culture of contentment" is rooted in us: the notion that those who are well integrated to the market "are doing nothing less than getting what they fairly deserve" and therefore "if their good fortune is deserved or if it is a reward for their personal merit, there is no plausible justification for any action that might either harm or inhibit it, that might reduce what is or may be enjoyed."[5] The other side of the coin is that the poor themselves are to blame for their own poverty and really deserve to be poor. Therefore, the current concentrating and excluding market mechanisms are seen as "incarnations" of a transcendental judge and justice. This is a secularized version of the retribution theology, so much criticized by Jesus and by the reformers through grace theology. In more ecclesiastic environments this modern religious version is referred to as prosperity theology.

Social inequality is now seen by many not only as inevitable and fair but also as beneficial. To Neo-liberals, with their unshakeable faith on the market, social inequality is the powerhouse of economic progress because it not only encourages competition between people

---

[5] Galbraith, John Kenneth, *A cultura do contentamento* (The Culture of Contentment), São Paulo, Pioneira, 1992, 12.

but also results from a competition-based society. In addition, social crisis, that is usually seen as temporary, is to them a sign that the economy is going in the right direction to full market freedom.

Based on the misunderstanding of identifying economic growth with human and social development, the economic and cultural leaders of today propose the modernization of economy and society as a whole as the only solution. Modernizing is understood in the sense of reducing all discussions and actions in the economic and political fields in terms of instrumental reasoning, that is, removing from the debate all humans and social values, people's and countries' rights and duties that come before (in the logical and chronological sense) the market system, and reducing everything to a matter of effectiveness in the relation between the scarce means and the economic goal of unlimited accumulation of wealth.

That is the reason why Roberto Campos, one of Brazil's former Ministers of the Economy and a staunch defender of Neo-liberalism, says that modernization, the only viable solution for Latin America, "assumes a *cruel mystique* of performance and the worship of efficiency."[6]

How can a mystique be cruel? Mystique is the force that makes us overcome the temptations of sin. And what is the fundamental sin in the opinion of neo-liberals? To them the essential and originating cause for economic and social evil (the original sin) is the economists' "pretension of knowledge"[7] of the market, that underlies all State interference and social movements seeking solutions to social problems. Wanting to consciously and intentionally solve social problems

---

[6] Campos, Roberto, *Além do cotidiano (Beyond everyday life)*, Rio de Janeiro: Record, 2nd. ed., 1985.

[7] Hayek, Fredrich A. von, "A pretensão do conhecimento" (The pretension of knowledge) *Humanidades*, vol. II, n. 5, Oct-Dec/83, Brasília: UnB, 47-54. This is the lecture delivered by F. Hayek when he was awarded the Economics Nobel Prize.

is seen as *the* sin which originates all other economic and social problems.

Neo-liberals claim that the only solution is to have faith on the market's "invisible hand," and see the suffering of the excluded as "necessary sacrifices" required by the laws of the market. For this reason, the mystique that should help us overcome the temptation of doing good things has a cruel face. It comes hand-in-hand with worshipping not the God of Mercy and Life but market efficiency.

The Good News of a God that is Love.

Faced with a world that experiences the "idolatry of the market," what "good news" should we announce to remain faithful to the gospel?

The criticism to market idolatry implies a criticism to the "sacredness" of the market and its laws. It means revealing the spirit of worshipping an idol—the work of human and social actions and interrelations raised to the category of god—that continually demands the sacrifice of human lives for the sake of wealth accumulation and endless consumption. Showing that the root of all types of economic and social evil is not our fight to live in a more humane and fair society but as the apostle Paul teaches us: "the love of money is the root of all kinds of evil (1 Tm 6:10)."

We have to recover a simple and irrefutable truth: the economy must exist for the sake of people's lives, and not people for the sake of economic laws based on the goal of accumulating wealth. This is one of the most important manners to translate the teachings of Jesus into the language of today: "The Sabbath was made for man, and not man for the Sabbath (Mark 2:27)."

The excluded from our societies are not only hungry for bread but also for their humanity which was denied, and for God. They hunger for a God who does not exclude anyone (cf. Acts 10:35 and Rom. 2:11), and who lives among human beings so "that they may have life, and that they may have it more abundantly (John 10:10)." For this good news to bear fruit in our society we must face our fundamental problem, that is the theological task of Churches: criticizing retribution theology, in the version of the "culture of contentment," and prosperity theology, because such theology sees sacredness in the injustice "of the world," by announcing a god (an idol) who legitimizes the culture of insensibility and blames its victims. To achieve it, we must return to grace theology. We must show that God is not behind all suffering and injustice; neither is He the provider of wealth for minorities; we must announce that God does not save us because of our merits, but because of his grace. And if we want to live according to the grace of our Lord, we will have to recognize, freely, beyond the market logic, the right of all people to have a real possibility of living a good and decent life. In other words, this means recovering the value of solidarity.

In sociologic terms, we are talking about a society that includes all. A world which contains many worlds, where the different, "the Jews and gentiles" learn to respect the differences and the equal right of everyone to live decently. Undoubtedly, such society will be one where the market is an important component of the economy. However, the market will be neither sacred nor almighty. There will be State and social democratic mechanisms to control and supplement market mechanisms, so that each individual's basic rights are respected and the ecological system is preserved.

Fighting for a society that includes everyone does not mean having an "a priori" political and economic project, but rather applying this principle as a criterion for discernment between several possible global or partial projects. The major point is no longer to be for or against a society model, but to see if and to what extent concrete models and proposals will help or prevent us from building a society where all may live a decent life.

Finally, another important point should me mentioned. In a globalised world, solutions to our problems should not be considered in local and national terms only. Articulation and co-ordination are required on an international level. This is another point where Christian Churches may render an important service to mankind. Christian Churches and international ecumenical bodies are some of the few institutions provided with both an international and local network, and which are concerned with the life of the poor and the excluded in the Americas. It is up to us to use our infrastructure and connections as best as possible so that life, the "blow of the Spirit" that inhabits all human beings, the great gift of God, is defended in its dignity and integrity.

Jung Mo Sung is a Catholic theologian and Professor of a graduate course on Sciences of Religion at the Methodist University and the Catholic University in São Paulo, Brazil.